GIANTS
of the
FAITH

GIANTS
of the
FAITH

*Classic Christian Writings
and the Men Behind Them*

RAYMOND BROWN

CROSSWAY BOOKS • WHEATON, ILLINOIS
A DIVISION OF GOOD NEWS PUBLISHERS

Library of Congress Cataloging-in-Publication Data
Brown, Raymond, 1928-
  Giants of the faith : classic Christian writings and the men behind them / Raymond Brown. —1st U.S. ed.
      p.   cm.
  Includes bibliographical references.
  ISBN 0-89107-987-4
  1. Spiritual life—Christianity. I. Title.
BV4501.2.B76676   1998
270'.092'2—dc21   97-39241

11	10	09	08	07	06	05	04	03	02	01	00	99	98
15	14	13	12	11	10	9	8	7	6	5	4	3	2	1

CONTENTS

Among the Shining Lights

Rising costs have created the DIY era. Many have responded adventurously to the challenge to "do it yourself." In doing so, some have had fun, even discovering hidden talents. Others, like me, still sigh for the craftsmen. There is, however, no such thing as a "DIY Christian." Nobody has all the gifts. Believers are meant to live interdependently. Paul's graphic illustration asserts that every part of the body relies on the cooperating function of other organs and limbs (1 Cor. 12:4-31). He told the Corinthians that, in the same way, every Christian needs the support and partnership of other believers. The totally independent, self-made Christian is a contradiction in terms.

George Herbert put it graphically to seventeenth-century ministers when he urged them to read books by other Christians. Just as no limb in the human body has all the functions, so likewise, he said, no nation has all the resources. God has planned it like that so that we can live, in measure, dependent on the help of each other:

> As one country does not bear all things, that there may be a commerce, so neither has God opened, or will open, all to one, that there may be a traffic in knowledge between the servants of God, for the planting both of love and humility.

Just as no country has all the resources, so no century has all the graces. George Herbert rightly insisted that "God in all ages has had his servants."[1] If we maintain that we have nothing to learn from them, we despise their love and endanger our humility.

The distinguishing hallmark of a healthy Christian is the desire to be a better one, and in the encouragement of Christian growth we have a great deal to learn from our partners who have gone ahead of us. They are not people left far behind, lost in a remote past, but our fellow believers, now alive in Christ, colleagues who have gone ahead of us to that better life that God has prepared for all who trust him. They have bequeathed penetrating insights, wide knowledge and rich experience. To dismiss them as irrelevant is due either to ignorance of who they were or arrogance about who we are.

Each of the four Christians I am privileged to introduce lived at a difficult time in history. Life was far from easy for any of them, but they lived heroically, resourcefully and effectively for Christ. For all their mistakes, the world was better because they were around. All four wrote many books, and I have selected a well-known one from each because, from different perspectives, I believe they have an immense amount to give to us in our quest to be better Christians in a not-so-different world.

The saintly Richard Baxter, who experienced imprisonment and innumerable hardships, and who scarcely knew a day without pain, wrote about "the profitable and pleasant company and help, at all times" he had found in Christian books. In dark times, they had enriched his mind and uplifted his spirit: "I have dwelt among the shining lights, which the learned, wise and holy men of all ages have set up, and left to illuminate the world."[2]

We shall look at four Christian classics that, among the many writings of each author, are distinctive in this sense: these believers here share their *personal* experience of the grace of God, the reality of Christ and the power of the indwelling Spirit. Jesus tells us that these men are not dead but more alive than they have ever been (John 11:25-26). One day, in God's mercy, we shall meet them. Their books begin a conversation that continues in heaven.

✝

AUGUSTINE

Confessions

You Were There Before Me

The ancient seaport of Hippo Regius was not an easy place to be a bishop. During the fourth century, the Christian community in North Africa was torn by bitter division, and rival churches were on opposite sides of the street. The man dragooned into the church's leadership at Hippo became one of the greatest Christians of all time. Prior to commencing this new phase in his life, this gifted scholar, Aurelius Augustinus, lived with a group of friends in a small monastic-type community in the town, having only recently moved there from Thagaste, now Souk Ahras in eastern Algeria. Thagaste in the Roman province of Numidia was his birthplace in a.d. 354, though in his late twenties he had left Africa for Italy in the hope of gaining a significant post in one of its leading cities. His mother, Monica, a devout Christian, longed that above all else her son might become a committed Christian, a concern not shared by her unbelieving husband, Patricius, whose only ambition for Augustine was for him to find some lucrative administrative or teaching position in the Roman world.

Monica's desire for her son's spiritual welfare probably bordered on maternal possessiveness. Something other than ambition may have driven the young man from his homeland. Given her strong religious and moral convictions, she certainly disapproved of his lifestyle, particularly his steady cohabitation with a young African girl, especially when she bore him a son, Adeodatus ("gift of God").

On the day he sailed with his girlfriend and son from Africa, Monica was devastated, though she clung to the hope that things might change. She did not know the whole of the story. The restless traveller's journeys and subsequent contacts were providentially directed, and in a new environment he was brought to clear personal faith. On a summer day in 386, he entered a garden in Milan with his close friend Alypius and, while reading one of Paul's epistles, experienced a dramatic personal encounter with Christ. It had not happened overnight. A wide variety of different events all played their part long before he entered that garden where, at a specific moment, an unsteady faith became sharply focused on the certainty of transforming personal experience. About thirteen years after his conversion, he wanted to place on record his indebtedness to God, and so he devoted time to writing what was to become a spiritual classic, his *Confessions*. The book has a threefold plan: It is an adoring conversation with God, a salutary message for himself and a persuasive testimony to others.

Although Augustine is distanced from us by a millennium and a half of revolutionising history, his writings must not be dismissed as irrelevant, merely of interest to those who dabble in the story of ancient cultures. We might be in danger of relegating him to an antiquated past unless we realise that his world was not so different from our own. It was a society noted for violence, superstition, occultism, subtle forms of idolatry, the proliferation of sects, the fear of death, family breakdown, child abuse and racial tensions— separated from late twentieth-century society by time and little else.

The local North African people were of a fiery and volatile temperament, and there were regular occasions when, as bishop, he had to meet a local official or legal representative to sort out a quarrel either within a family or between neighbours, or legislate concerning a charge of injustice over some business transaction or other. Augustine loved to preach (a thousand sermons survive), but his daily work included a wide range of other responsibilities such as visiting the sick at a time when most of the highly superstitious locals were specially vulnerable and, afraid of illness, could easily be caught up with occult activities. He gave a considerable amount of time to writing letters (we can still read a couple hundred of them) and also helped the Christians of his day by producing books that expounded Scripture, explained doctrine, encouraged devotion, addressed problems of faith and combated heresy.

During his busy life he wrote over a hundred books—so many that a later bishop, Isidore of Seville, said that if anyone claimed to have read everything written by Augustine, he was probably stretching the truth. Before a new book had sufficient time to reach any part of the Christian world, another was on its way. Some were relatively short, others massive. One of them, the *City of God*, took him about thirteen years to write and, though wordy, remains a monumental study of a contrast that is still important; that is, the contrast between the transitory nature of the city that represents this world's achievements and the permanent character of God's sovereign purposes, the city that lasts forever. That book was written as the proud empire that arrogantly described itself as "eternal Rome" was in process of disintegration, helplessly overrun by the barbarian hordes. At the end of Augustine's life, they took over the whole of that North African coast, and his "tale of two cities" contained a message of striking relevance: When all else decays, remember that the things of God last forever. But here we turn to his other famous work, the *Confessions*.

It is a brilliantly written book; to explore it is to discover rich veins of graphic autobiography, social history, psychological insight, biblical interpretation and spiritual perception. Our immediate purpose is to narrow our interest to one specific aim—to look at Augustine's classic work as a rich expression of Christian spirituality and to learn from this outstanding Christian how we can deepen our relationship with God and achieve our potential as his adoring children, obedient servants and effective witnesses in the contemporary world. Three huge themes dominate the *Confessions*—knowing God, admitting need and receiving help.

KNOWING GOD

At no point do the *Confessions* profess to be simple autobiography. The title indicates a twofold purpose: It is a confession of faith and a confession of need. From its opening words we realise that we are in the company of a man on his knees, openly acknowledging that in the presence of God he is seeker, pauper and debtor. Addressed clearly to God, the book is one sustained, deeply sincere prayer. Its first paragraph, containing its most quoted sentence, captures Augustine's sense of wonder and gratitude:

> You are great, Lord, and highly to be praised . . . to praise you is the desire of man, a little piece of your creation. You stir man to take pleasure in praising you, because you have made us for yourself, and our heart is restless until it rests in you.[1]

As he writes, Augustine enters God's presence so that he might discern something more of the Lord's greatness; in the *Confessions* we are with a praying man who is making fresh, exciting and humbling discoveries about the nature of God. Nobody can make progress in spiritual maturity without a constantly enriched understanding of God. Yet Augustine knows that men and women cannot simply determine to know God with the mere aid of their limited rational processes. Three issues come to prominence here, and Augustine realised their importance in his quest for a personal experience of God—the limitation of our intellectual resources, the devastation wrought in those rational processes by human sin, and our total reliance upon God, who will use but also transcend our best mental equipment by revealing himself to us personally.

The first issue concerns the limitation of our intellectual resources in the search for God. Augustine had a first-class mind, but he came to see that men and women cannot know God simply by subscribing to a series of intellectual propositions about him. Personal quest and pastoral experience alike demonstrated that if anyone is to come to God, then reason must be joined by both emotion and will. On the threshold of conversion he testified to man's limited intellectual ability. His friend Alypius listened in stunned silence as Augustine painfully contrasted the joy of faith experienced by illiterate people with the spiritual barrenness of scholars like himself, who could engage in lengthy discussions about God but are left not knowing him personally: "What is wrong with us? ... Uneducated people are rising up and capturing heaven, and we with our high culture *without any heart*—see where we roll in the mud of flesh and blood."[2]

He knew that while he must be intellectually persuaded about the Christian faith, the emotions had to be involved as well; there must be a passionate desire to know God if he was to come to radiant personal faith. His will must also be surrendered in submissive obedience.

But, second, even if he had the desire, the search might not be easy. In the quest for God, the rational processes are not only limited; they are also impaired. Augustine discovered that in the pursuit of spiritual reality his agile mind was a labyrinth of confused ideas, and, like all else in his personality, the choice gift of human rationality had been perverted and distorted by sin. He was seeking to know God—but on his own terms, in his own time and by his own means. His imaginative mind was constantly diverted to sensual priorities; he had been sidetracked into false ideas about God; his intellectualism had become idolatrous and infected by pride; and the Bible, the very book that alone could bring him to God, he had hastily dismissed as inferior literature. The opening section of the *Confessions* gives eloquent expression to his need of help beyond himself:

> Have mercy so that I may find words. . . . Speak to me that I may hear. . . . The house of my soul is too small for you to come to it. May it be enlarged by you. It is in ruins: restore it. In your eyes it has offensive features. I admit it, I know it; but who will clean it up?[3]

The third issue Augustine comes to recognise is that however deeply men and women desire personal faith, they will never know

God unless he reveals himself to them. From boyhood onwards, Augustine had been deeply religious, but he came to see that in seeking God we can amass a considerable amount of religious information but still not know him personally. In the opening section of the *Confessions*, Augustine confesses human inadequacy by giving expression to a range of urgent questions that, one after another, rise to the surface of his constantly probing mind:

> But who calls upon you when he does not know you? . . . How shall I call upon my God? . . . Where may he come to me? . . . Who then are you, my God? . . . What has anyone achieved in words when he speaks about you? . . . In your mercies, Lord God, tell me what you are to me.[4]

Without God, life's baffling questions remain unanswered. Only with help from beyond himself can Augustine begin to understand where he has come from, why he is here or where he is going. Life's origin, meaning and destiny are mysteries that God alone can unfold.

Desperate to find the answers to such huge, perplexing questions, and realising that he might search forever without meeting God, he pleads that God will reveal himself to him. God honours the desperate man or woman who calls upon him in utter reliance, and because Augustine comes dependently, his long quest is rewarded with illuminating insights into the nature of the God he longs to know. With exultant gratitude Augustine uses the *Confessions* to adore a God who speaks, loves and waits.

God Speaks

We have already seen that the book begins with a series of urgent questions that burst anxiously from the mind of a bewildered seeker. Yet alongside the questions are their illuminating answers in Scripture, and from the first sentence to the last, Augustine weaves carefully chosen biblical quotations into the rich tapestry of his narrative. In many places the unfolding paragraphs become a pattern of Scripture verses, skillfully set alongside each other so that one comments meaningfully on another, until at the close of the book he gives himself to the sustained interpretation of a key passage at the beginning of Genesis.

The Bible is at the heart of Augustine's believing experience. Gifted preacher that he is, he longs that, as well as his sermons, this book also might take its readers to the word of God in both Old and New Testaments. He knew that genuine seekers might find a problem just there. In the culture of his day, sophisticated thinkers looked for the answer to life's profound questions in the pages of erudite philosophical writings but not in the Scriptures of the Christian church. These were regarded by intellectuals as extremely poor literature. When Augustine first began to read the Bible seriously, he was appalled. In those days he was a youth of eighteen, studying rhetoric at Carthage, and words were the tools of his trade. It was exceptionally important for an argument to be presented not only intelligently and lucidly but attractively as well. It must appeal to the mind, move the heart and persuade the will, and with such conventions uppermost in his mind, the Bible seemed poor stuff. He considered that it was

> . . . unworthy in comparison with the dignity of Cicero. My inflated conceit shunned the Bible's restraint, and my gaze never penetrated to its inwardness. Yet the Bible was composed in such a way that as beginners mature, its meaning grows with them. I disdained to be a little beginner. Puffed up with pride, I considered myself a mature adult.

Too arrogant to submit himself to the biblical message, Augustine preferred something more polished from a literary perspective, less taxing in its moral demands, more accommodating to the thought forms of his age. He came to realise that only the humble receive the message of Scripture. Its message is not "open to the proud" and, he says, "I was not in any state . . . to bow my head to climb its steps."[5]

It was through the biblical expositions of Ambrose, the gifted preacher in Milan, that Augustine came to see that a man with an excellent mind could not only appreciate but be changed by the Bible. With this confidence in Scripture firmly established, it was only a step to the profound discovery that the Christ of Scripture could transform his life. Words from Paul's letter to the Romans came to him in the peace of that Milan garden with compelling assurance:

> So I hurried back to the place where Alypius was sitting. There I had put down the book of the apostle when I got up. I seized it, opened it and in silence read the first passage on which my eyes lit: "Not in riots and drunken parties, not in eroticism and indecencies, not in strife and rivalry, but put on the Lord Jesus Christ and make no provision for the flesh in its lusts" (Rom 13:13-14). I neither wished nor needed to read further. At once, with the last words of this sentence, it was as if a light of relief from all anxiety flooded into my heart. All the shadows of doubt were dispelled.[6]

From that moment on, Augustine was, in Luther's phrase, "captive to the Word." When in 391, totally against his personal wishes, he was appointed presbyter in the church at Hippo, he begged his bishop to allow him an initial period of study—leave to improve his knowledge of the Bible. He had been persuaded "to accept the post next to the helmsman" before he had "even learned to handle an oar."[7] Time with the Scriptures would be the best possible preparation for his new work.

Augustine is telling us that there can be no development in Christian spirituality unless we accept the unique message God has given us in Scripture. To adore him is to honour a God who speaks; such reverence means bringing a daily attentiveness to his Word and our willing submission to its teaching.

God Loves

Moreover, this speaking God has a message of infinite tenderness. His first word is love; that is his name, and that is his nature.

Augustine discovered it to be a love that provides, pursues, protects and pardons.

In his exposition of the loving provision of God, Augustine uses the *Confessions* to reflect on his earliest days. The message that came through to him from the experience of infancy was that God's compassion contrasts sharply with human sin. Unfolding his story, he reflects on what life must have been like for him at the very beginning. He thanks God for the miracle by which he was consistently and lovingly fed:

> So I was welcomed with the consolations of human milk, but it was not my mother or my nurses who made any decision to fill their breasts, but you who through them gave me infant food, in accordance with your ordinance and the riches which are distributed deep in the natural order. . . . Indeed all good things come from you, O God, and "from my God is all my salvation." (2 Sam 23:5)[8]

Moreover, this love of God is not confined to infancy; it pursued him through childhood and adult experience. He constantly testifies to that loving hand behind so many events in his young life. God did more than feed a loving, dependent child; he persistently followed an arrogantly independent, morally perverse adult, and did so with infinite compassion. This theme of the patient, seeking, inescapable love of God is never far from his mind: "I travelled along the broad way of the world, but you did not desert me."[9]

In his pursuit, God is not remotely deterred by our stubborn determination to keep him at bay:

> The closed heart does not shut out your eye, and your hand is not kept away by the hardness of humanity, but you melt that when you wish, either in mercy or in punishment, and there is "none who can hide from your heat." . . . You alone are always present even to those who have taken themselves far from you. . . . You were there before me, but . . . I could not even find myself, much less you.[10]

He also came to see that he was not only pursued but protected, even during those times when he had no regard for God. A loving God was his moral guardian, hedging him about with bulwarks of defensive compassion, keeping him back from contagious sins and destructive transgression:

> I also attribute to your grace whatever evil acts I have *not* done. What could I not have done when I loved gratuitous crime? I confess that everything has been forgiven, both the evil things I did of my own accord, and those which I did not do because of your guidance.
>
> No one who considers his frailty would dare attribute to his own strength his chastity and innocence, so that he has less cause to love you—as if he had less need of your mercy. . . . He should love you no less, indeed even more; for he sees that the one who has delivered me from the great sicknesses of my sins is also he through whom he may see that he himself has not been a victim of the same great sicknesses.[11]

God had not only pursued Augustine in his godlessness and protected him from sins that might ruin him; he had also met him generously when, despite persistent warnings, he did sin. Though he had revelled in his iniquity, God forgave him when he cried for pardon—such was his unmerited compassion. So Augustine prays:

> I will love you, Lord, and will give thanks and confession to your name because you have forgiven me such great evils and my nefarious deeds. I attribute to your grace and mercy that you have melted my sins away like ice.[12]

God Waits

In the *Confessions*, Augustine frequently marvels at the patience of God who knows the right time to speak and act. Unwilling to be hurried, he is ready to wait for the best moment, though it may be long delayed. Augustine writes about God's deliberate "silences" when he seems to be doing nothing but is really calmly biding his time, knowing that at some future date there will be a better opportunity for him to intervene. Meanwhile, he is willing to be ignored, misunderstood, dismissed, even ridiculed, all in the interests of a future conquest. During his youth Augustine "ran wild in the shadowy jungle of erotic adventures," but God waited patiently for his return:

> I travelled very far from you, and you did not stop me. I was tossed about and spilt, scattered and boiled dry in my fornications. And you were silent. How slow I was to find my joy. . . . At that time you said nothing, and I travelled much further away from you into more and more sterile things productive of unhappiness . . . incapable of rest in my exhaustion.[13]

As the years went by, God silently eroded those things that had been this man's sole delight. He created within Augustine's sensitive mind a holy dissatisfaction, which became more unbearable as the months went by. It was God's gentle way of bringing him to acknowledge his need and total helplessness. God patiently closed doors, so that he would be left with only one way to turn:

> I aspired to honours, money, marriage, and you laughed at me. In those ambitions I suffered the bitterest difficulties; that was by your mercy—so much the greater in that you gave me the less occasion to find sweet pleasure in what was not you.[14]

An experienced pastor, Augustine knew that anyone who wants to know God needs something in addition to a reliable portraiture of the divine nature. The genuine seeker must have a realistic view of himself as well as a persuasive concept of God. Augustine makes no secret of his sins, not because he wants his contemporaries to know the intellectual arrogance and moral depravity of a North African youth, but because he genuinely believes that his experience is not unique. Others may not sin in the manner he did, but all his readers are transgressors, and sin must be exposed and acknowledged before men and women can experience the grace of a forgiving God. It is for this theological reason that he uses the *Confessions* to unfold a story not simply about Augustine of Thagaste, but of Everyman and Everywoman in his world and ours.

ADMITTING NEED

Augustine wrote his book as a prayer of gratitude to God, and that sense of adoring wonder never left him. Later in life he said that he was as deeply moved when he read the *Confessions* as he was when he wrote them. He feared that his book might be devoured merely by readers with an unhealthy curiosity about his youthful adventures: "The human race is inquisitive about other people's lives, but negligent to correct their own."[15] He prays that his book will fall into the hands of despairing people who also need forgiveness and hope:

> Stir up the heart when people read and hear the confessions of my past wickednesses, which you have forgiven and covered up to grant me happiness in yourself. . . . Prevent their heart from sinking into the sleep of despair and saying, "It is beyond my power." On the contrary, the heart is aroused in the love of your mercy and by the sweetness of your grace, by which every weak person is given power, while dependence on grace produces awareness of one's own weakness.[16]

It is this stark, honest exposure that makes the *Confessions* such compelling reading. We see ourselves as we really are only when confronted by this holy, yet loving God. Then we know that we are arrogant, rebellious and unfulfilled people, desperately in need of God's transforming work in our lives.

We Are Arrogant

The sin above all sins that dominates the *Confessions* is not sexual desire or practice; it is human pride, a basic transgression frankly confessed in every one of Books I to IX. Pride corrupted his boyhood friendships, controlled his student ambitions, shaped his adult values and determined his religious reading, so that it offended his cultural dignity to study the Bible. How can God reach men and women infected by pride at almost every level of their lives? He does it by astonishing them in the Incarnation. At the beginning of the *Confessions* Augustine praises God for the gift of faith. How it came to such a self-important intellectual snob was a miracle of mercy: "You breathed it into me by the humanity of your Son, by the ministry of your preacher."[17]

In other words, Ambrose spoke persuasively to him about Jesus. Augustine knows that we can only receive forgiveness through the redeeming work of Christ upon the cross, a theme he expounds eloquently elsewhere in his writings, but the aspect of Christ's person and work that dominates the *Confessions* is that of our Lord's attractive humanity and transformingly effective humility. His gratitude for the person of Christ is credal and lyrical as he shares how he was delivered from introverted pride, encouraging the most despondent reader to seek the same release:

> You sent him [the true Mediator] so that from his example they should learn humility. . . . He appeared among mortal sinners as the immortal righteous one, mortal like humanity, righteous like God. . . . For us he was victorious before you and victor because he was victim. For us before you he is priest and sacrifice, and priest because he is sacrifice. Before you he makes us sons instead of servants by being born of you and being servant to us. With good reason my firm hope is in him. For you will cure all my diseases through him who sits at your right hand and intercedes with you for us. Otherwise I would be in despair.[18]

Augustine is too realistic to suggest that pride vanishes at conversion. He often preached about the triple enemy in 1 John 2:16; the third, "the pride of life" (KJV), was the most sinister foe. He confessed:

> Surely the third kind of temptation has not ceased to trouble me, nor during the whole of this life can it cease. . . . The temptation is to wish to be feared or loved by people for no reason other than the joy derived from such power, which is no joy at all.[19]

Human pride can be vanquished only by the humility and self-offering of Christ. Arrogant and self-satisfied, we stand aloof from him, proudly clutching the shabby rags of our poor achievements. Yet for us he joyfully relinquished the splendour of eternity so that he might pursue us in love:

> He who for us is life itself descended here and endured our death and slew it by the abundance of his life. . . . He did not delay, but ran crying out loud by his words, deeds, death, life, descent, ascent—calling us to return to him.

The Incarnation becomes a model for the penitent's return to a holy God. We must abandon all thought that by our intellectual acumen, religious knowledge or moral superiority we can ascend to God. Such a way is not open to us. Every person must descend from the pinnacle of self-reliant pride, kneeling in dependent humility. If we are honest, the pinnacle is a proud illusion; life's sins have brought us low enough, and there is little to boast about: "Come down so that you can ascend. . . . For it is by climbing up against God that you have fallen."[20]

Only Christ can dislodge us from the pinnacle of pride, and it was a long time before Augustine acknowledged it. Obsessed with the notion that he might discover the truth by rigourous philosophical enquiry, he read, searched, pondered and discussed, but to "possess my God, the humble Jesus, I was not yet humble enough. I did not know what his weakness was meant to teach." In time, Augustine came to see that:

> Your Word [Christ], eternal truth . . . raises those submissive to him to himself . . . they are no longer to place confidence in themselves but rather to become weak. They see at their feet divinity become weak by his sharing in our "coat of skin." In their weariness they fall prostrate before this divine weakness which rises and lifts them up.[21]

We Are Rebellious

This selfless, incarnate Lord was sent not only to humble the proud but to transform the rebel. Sin is more than intellectual arrogance, the persistent refusal to consider God's perspective on our lives; it is destructive warfare, deliberately intent on disobeying what God has said. It is this aspect of human sin that presses the message of the *Confessions* home with compelling power: It is not only sin against God but also, consequently and inevitably, sin against others. In the famous incident of the pear tree, Augustine relates an experience from his youth that is a flagrant illustration of human sinfulness. Once again, we are in a garden, not this time where light bursts forth, but where darkness reigns. This garden is plundered by youths intent on stealing pears, not because they are hungry but because they delight in doing what is forbidden. Augustine freely confesses they had superior pears at home; they stole only to destroy, and the very act of destruction gave them immense pleasure. In recalling his experience, Augustine exposes the wanton sinfulness of Everyman. Sin is forbidden, egocentric, malevolent and corporate.

Sin is forbidden; it is a wilful offence against God: "Our pleasure lay in doing what was not allowed." "Was it possible," he asks, "to take pleasure in what was illicit for no reason other than that it was not allowed?" The young thieves knew it was wrong to steal; that was a law of God, available even to those who knew nothing of the Ten Commandments, being a law "written in the hearts of men which not even iniquity itself destroys." Even the inveterate thief is incensed when someone filches his belongings. He invents excuses for his own behaviour but cannot tolerate anyone who steals his property, "even if he is rich and the other is destitute."

Sin is egocentric. Self-love was of surpassing importance as those youths plundered the fruit:

> I became evil for no reason. I had no motive for my wickedness except wickedness itself. It was foul and I loved it. I loved the self-destruction. I loved my fall, not the object for which I had fallen but my fall itself. . . . I was not seeking to gain anything by shameful means, but shame for its own sake. . . . I threw away what I had picked solely with the motive of stealing. . . . If any of those pears entered my mouth, my criminality was the piquant sauce.

Sin is malevolent. The offenders were ruthlessly intent on depriving another person of his possessions. Late at night, Augustine and his friends "carried off a huge load of pears . . . merely to throw to the pigs." They had no thought whatever for the owner of the tree: "Out of a game and a jest came an avid desire to do injury and an appetite to inflict loss on someone else."

Sin is corporate. It was not a solitary act of vandalism but one made more compellingly attractive because he was in the company of others. Though self-pleasure excluded almost all else from his mind that night, one other thought invaded his thinking as with rapturous enjoyment he stripped the tree of its fruit: "I remember my state of mind to be thus at the time—alone I would never have done it. . . . It was all done for a giggle. . . . Friendship can be a dangerous enemy."

Here again, pride plays its part: "As soon as the words are spoken, 'Let us go and do it,' one is ashamed not to be shameless."

The scenario was degrading, but the offence is deliberately heightened and the story presented in profound theological terms. Tree, fruit and fall have intense spiritual significance; the story in

Genesis 3 is never far from the writer's mind. Critics of the narrative, like Oliver Wendell Holmes ("Rum thing to see a man making a mountain out of robbing a pear tree in his teens") have scarcely begun to understand what Augustine was writing about when, using the context of youthful destruction, he depicts the tragic sinfulness of the human condition. His use of the "fruit" imagery is particularly striking, recalling the apostle's piercing question in Romans: "What benefit did you reap at that time from the things you are now ashamed of? Those things result in death."

The unwanted fruit had been thrown to the pigs; it was over and done with. The night escapade passed, but its effects remained. Damage had been done, not simply to the tree and its owner, but to the thief; fruit remained that could not be jettisoned like stolen pears: "What fruit had I, wretched boy, in these things (Rom 6:21) which I now blush to recall, above all in that theft in which I loved nothing but the theft itself?"[22]

Augustine becomes passionate not only in his exposure of sin, but in his exposition of grace. Even rebels can be changed, and one crucial factor in their transformation is an increasing sense of dissatisfaction; that persistent sense of emptiness is a gift of God, as Everyman discovers when each successive rebellious act offers only transitory pleasure, and he is left increasingly destitute, aching for something better.

We Are Unfulfilled

Everyman is proud and rebellious, but for all that, he is spiritually unique, made in the divine image. There is a God-shaped vacuum in every human life and Augustine's famous opening saying is eloquent about our deepest spiritual need—God himself: "You have made us for yourself, and our heart is restless until it rests in you." Only he can fill the cavernous emptiness with true and lasting satisfaction. As Henry Chadwick says, "Augustine's sentence announces a major theme of the work."[23]

The opening of the book reveals not only an admission of restlessness, but a yearning for rest: "Who will enable me to find rest in you? Who will grant that you come to my heart and intoxicate it, so that I forget my evils and embrace my one and only good, yourself?"[24]

Augustine perceives that the discovery of true rest in God can only come as alternative values become less attractive. God alone can diminish their fascination, minimise their appeal and expose their transient worth. The Genesis Fall narrative is the most influential Old Testament passage in the *Confessions*, and it is to the prodigal son that Augustine looks for his New Testament portraiture of Everyman's loss and gain. He hints at Luke's parable at the close of his opening chapter, recalling how he "was swept along by vanities and travelled right away from you, my God."[25] As the tale unfolds, the rebel becomes a runaway, but he will never long for home until the fascinations of the far country have been seen for what they are. Augustine concludes the story of his orchard theft with an admission of his distance from a generous Father: "As an adolescent I went astray from you, my God. . . . I became to myself a region of destitution."[26]

In his student days in Carthage, "a cauldron of illicit loves," he longed to love and be loved, but it was a hunger no human relationship could satisfy. Something within always sighed for more: "My hunger was internal, deprived of inward food, that is of you yourself, my God." His natural appetites masked a spiritual need, and it was some time before he confessed that the inward craving could only be met by God. The prodigal still had money in his purse, and until that ran out, he would continue his search for deeper satisfaction:

> I was without any desire for incorruptible nourishment . . . the emptier I was, the more unappetizing such food became. So my soul was in rotten health. In an ulcerous condition it thrust itself to outward things. . . . Yet physical things had no soul. . . . My God, my mercy, in your goodness you mixed in much vinegar with that sweetness.[27]

God is not aloof, standing at a detached distance, waiting for the prodigal to return; he is in the far country, searching him out: "Look where he is—wherever there is a taste of truth. He is very close to the heart, but the heart has wandered from him. . . . Rest in him and you will be at rest."[28]

Augustine's pursuit of satisfaction and rest is given eloquent expression early in the book as he retraces his steps in both philosophy and religion. Philosophy offers a partial answer to what he desires; religion, in his case Manichaeism, provides a misleading answer to his quest.

The philosophical approach takes him so far, but cannot provide the complete answer. In his quest for God, philosophy is like a signpost; it may point him in the right direction, but it cannot get him to his destination. In his case the initial waymark is a book, which he read during his student days, Cicero's *Hortensius*, "an exhortation to study philosophy." Its message to the young seeker was to pursue the quest for truth and let that be the controlling ambition of his life. In the "far country" God uses many things to create our sense of need, and we must not underestimate their importance. Augustine remained grateful for the day he was introduced to that book: "The book changed my feelings. It altered my prayers, Lord, to be towards yourself. It gave me different values and priorities. . . . *I began to rise up to return to you*."[29] The language anticipates the prodigal's decision.

Cicero's book contained an excellent message, but it could not get him far enough. His first response to it was to seek truth in the Bible, and, as we have seen, he did not like what he read. So, what next?

Augustine became a Manichee, a member of a weird sect whose name derived from Mani, a third-century guru. His teaching mixed what he considered to be the acceptable aspects of Christianity with speculative notions about creation, the evil nature of matter, the influence of the stars and the idea (fancifully recaptured in contemporary New Age teaching) that there are bits of God in all of us. Augustine was a "hearer" (as second-rank

Manichees were called), as opposed to the top-drawer "elect," but Manichaeism, with its inflated notions of religious self-importance, did little for his humility.

The Manichees claimed to be looking for the truth and were highly critical of the Bible Augustine had just dismissed; this made their ideas all the more appealing to him. Mani had spoken with authority, claiming to be a personification of the Holy Spirit. Augustine had just rejected a Spirit-inspired book, preferring a more palatable alternative. But the way of Mani took him into the "far country" for nine further years until that sense of emptiness became unbearably acute. Rest was not to be found among the Manichees; it was the preaching of Ambrose that gave him an appreciation of Scripture and pointed him to Christ, the unique way to God.

The mistake of travelling along the wrong path in the quest for spiritual truth is not remotely confined to the world of antiquity. Genuine seekers in our own time can be tragically misled. In Western society, new religions and deviant sects proliferate with every passing year. Thousands of our contemporaries find them compellingly attractive, especially when they encourage their devotees to bypass the Bible and be selective in their thinking about Jesus, discarding its teaching about his deity, virgin birth, and the necessity of his redeeming death.

There are lessons for modern seekers in Augustine's frustrating experience. Several of the new religions, like New Age thinking, have astonishing similarities with Manichaeism. Manichaeism claimed unique inspiration by the Holy Spirit. It displayed markedly syncretistic features, drawing its key ideas from a variety of other religions. It had a decidedly oriental flavour to its teaching. It presented a two-tier form of spirituality, offering a top-grade category for privileged ascetics. It discerned life's meaning from reading the stars. It maintained that there are particles of God in each of us, which by appropriate religious means can be released from their imprisoned state. Those who take the trouble to study the sects will find echoes of these features in many of the emergent

new religions in our contemporary Western culture. New Age
thinking adopts most of them. Augustine's religious world is only
different from ours in that we have more religions on offer than
could be conveniently pursued in fourth- and fifth-century North
Africa.

He gradually recognised that Manichaeism was a bankrupt
form of faith, but God allowed him to continue along that delusive
path so that he could see it for what it was—empty, devoid of truth,
spiritually unsatisfying. The quest for rest was not to be found in
Mani's message, any more than it is in modern deviations such as
Scientology, New Age, Eckankar, Transcendental Meditation, the
Divine Light Mission, the Unification Church ("Moonies") and
their like. Augustine portrayed his deluded religious quest as that
of a hungry man who sees appetising food in his dreams; it all
looked the same as real food, but it could only torment, never
satisfy:

> The dishes they placed before me contained splendid halluci-
> nations. . . . Nevertheless, because I took them to be you, I ate.
> . . . You were not those empty fictions, and I derived no nour-
> ishment from them but was left more exhausted than before.[30]

Yet God was present, even in the fruitless quest. Toward the
close of his book Augustine confesses, "You made me, and when I
forgot you, you did not forget me. . . . Before I called to you, you
were there before me."[31] In order to find rest, he must first admit
his spiritual starvation. Then he must look more critically at those
things that fail to meet his need, and only then will he realise that
in God alone is humanity's satisfying food.

Expanding the illustration of hallucinatory food seen in
dreams, he acknowledged that, however good the sleep, he woke
every day to the realisation that fantasy could never relieve the
hunger. Augustine said in his *Soliloquies*: "For I do not think that
these things of earth can sink to the utmost level of contempt in my
mind unless I see that reality in comparison with which these

things seem cheap."[32] He would only leave his illusions when he tasted excellent food that does not belong to a dream world.

God used a variety of means to enable Augustine to see the aridity of all other quests. The frustrating search had many painful facets—rebellion, disappointment, bewilderment, illness, bereavement, deprivation—but all were abundantly worthwhile if they brought him closer to the God who never abandons his search:

> By inward goads you stirred me to make me find it unendurable until, through my inward perception, you were a certainty to me . . . my mind's troubled and darkened eye, under the hot dressing of salutary sorrows, was . . . brought back to health.[33]

The best things in life cannot satisfy, let alone the worst:

> These inferior goods have their delights, but not comparable to my God who has made them all. It is in him that the just person takes delight; he is the joy of those who are true of heart.

We crave for things, but he alone is "the inexhaustible treasure of incorruptible pleasure." We greedily demand plenty; he possesses everything and gives it all away. He is everything that we are not, and the promised rest will certainly be found by those who turn dependently to him.[34]

He comes to us not because we deserve him, but because we need him. In one of his expositions of the Psalms, Augustine put it perfectly:

> It is not of our merits, but His free grace. What good have we sinners deserved? . . . Nevertheless, the Merciful One loved, the Bridegroom loved, not because she was beautiful, but that he might make her beautiful.[35]

RECEIVING HELP

In Augustine's book, we are privileged to travel with an earnest
seeker on a journey through the "inner space" of his spiritual quest,
but we soon realise that we are not in the presence of an insular indi-
vidualist; his experience is personal but not independent. He gratefully acknowledges the immense goodness of God and wants us to
know that grace has often been mediated through the lives of others.
The *Confessions* is a chronicle of debt, recalling how several people,
some in North Africa, others in Italy, were used to bring this outstanding thinker to vibrant personal faith. To look at their part in the
story is to remember that Christian spirituality is not pursued in isolation from our fellow believers; other people have a role in the story
of every Christian's development. A reflective look at Augustine's
friends may suggest how we might encourage others in the quest for
holiness.

Augustine's appreciation of his colleagues was unbounded. It
was held that Christian friendships were made in heaven,[36] but
experience taught him that some relationships are spawned in
hell. In childhood his contacts with older people were not always
happy.[37] The gang of youths to which he later belonged was certainly a damaging influence: "I . . . could not conceivably have
done it by myself." For further study he went to Carthage; the
scene was different but the behaviour worse. Groups of aggressive students ("The Wreckers"), intent on vandalism, also took
pleasure in inflicting as much physical hurt as possible, especially
on freshmen at university. Augustine did not share in their
destructive activity, but such was their power that he "lived
among them shamelessly ashamed of not being one of the
gang."[38]

When Augustine changed from student to teacher, he had
abundant evidence of the harmful potential of a group. On reaching Rome, his friend Alypius was soon lured back into the enjoyment of vicious and cruel entertainments by damaging friends. He
had begun to detest such spectacles, but

. . . some of his friends and fellow-pupils on their way back
from a dinner happened to meet him in the street, and despite
his energetic refusal and resistance, used friendly violence to
take him into the amphitheatre during the days of the cruel
and murderous games.[39]

Augustine tells the story for a spiritual purpose; many a good
Christian has suffered a severe setback because of the adverse
influence of a godless individual or group. From his pastoral experience at Hippo, Augustine knows that a wrong decision, made in
an unguarded moment, can create havoc in the life of a sensitive
man or woman.

Yet Augustine did not linger for long on the danger of bad relationships; he spent more time affirming the blessing of good ones,
and we shall turn to some of them now. In the course of his grateful testimony he shows how God used many people and different
experiences to bring him to personal faith.

A Mother's Prayers

Monica has an important role in the *Confessions*, yet although
Augustine is indebted to his devout mother, he does not eulogise
her at every turn. He is aware of her failings as well as her devotion, but in exposing her frailty, he is still helping his reader.

Describing Monica's spiritual and moral development, he tells
us that earlier in her life "a weakness for wine gradually got a grip
of her." On first tasting it, she heartily disliked it, but gradually
adding more sips every day, she got into the habit of "gulping
down almost full cups" of the stuff. Once again, to underline the
influence of others, he points out how an unsophisticated slave girl
was used to bring his mother sharply off the bottle. During a dis-
pute, the girl "insulted her by bringing up the accusation that she
was a boozer. The taunt hurt. She reflected upon her own foul
addiction, at once condemned it, and stopped the habit."
Augustine uses the story to make the point that "just as flattering

friends corrupt, so quarrelsome enemies often bring us correction."
The sovereign Lord was at work in Monica's early life: "But you,
Lord . . . turn to your own purposes the deep torrents. . . . Even from
the fury of one soul you brought healing to another."[40]

Monica married Patricius and did not have an easy life.
Sometimes he handled her very roughly indeed, but she knew how
to cope with him. She did so with such success that neighbours
abused by their husbands, women who "bore the marks of blows
and suffered disfigurement to their faces," came to talk to her in
their troubles and obtain her advice on how to live with an aggressive husband.[41]

Patricius did not become a Christian until later in life, but
Monica was a good example in their home and prayed both for him
and for their son's conversion. This aspect of her witness made a
deep impression on Augustine, and in relating the story, he offers
pastoral encouragement to parents whose children have not, as yet,
followed them in the faith.

Monica had every cause to be concerned when her son went off
to Carthage. Long before that he had boasted of sexual adventures,
though some of it was mere talk, mainly to impress his friends.
Away from the restraints of home, anything might happen; by that
time his father had died so Monica felt alone, weighed down by a
heavy sense of moral responsibility for her son. When, in addition
to taking a mistress, living with her, and eventually giving her a
child, he became a zealot for the teaching of the Manichees, her distress doubled. To moral deviancy he had added religious heresy. It
played so deeply on her mind that one night she dreamt about it,
and the dream brought her such comfort that she daringly shared
it with her wayward son.

In the dream, a "young man came to her, handsome, cheerful
and smiling to her at a time when she was sad and crushed with
grief." The young man asked why she was sad, and Monica told
him about her wayward son; he replied with this assurance—that
where she was, there Augustine was also. She then looked and saw
her son standing beside her. When she related the dream to

Augustine, he tauntingly retorted that it surely meant that she too would become a Manichee. With impressive speed, Monica replied: "The word spoken to me was not, 'Where he is, there you will be also,' but 'Where you are, there he will be also.'" Augustine was more deeply moved by his mother's quick response than by the dream itself. For nine years, he persisted as a Manichee, but Monica prayed on for his conversion. The dream had caused her to be "cheered by hope but no less constant in prayer."

Like other intercessors, she occasionally became impatient for an answer to her prayer and asked a particular bishop if he would talk to her son and expose the futility of his bizarre beliefs. She thought the man eminently suitable for the task, since earlier in life he too had been a Manichee, and a well-read one at that. To her great grief, the bishop was adamant; he would not speak with him. Monica was staggered, and she insisted he must. Irritated by her persistent pleading, the bishop said something that stayed with her and Augustine throughout their lives: "Go away from me; as you live, it cannot be that the son of these tears should perish." Augustine remembered that in later conversations "she often used to recall that she had taken those words as if they had sounded from heaven."[42]

Her experience as a believing intercessor was put to a severe test when Augustine decided to sail for Italy with his mistress and their son. Monica was distracted that she was losing her direct spiritual influence in his life and begged the Lord to prevent him from going to Rome. The sequence illustrates a spiritual principle of outstanding importance: Our prayers are not always answered in the way we hope. God refused to answer her urgent prayer because he wanted to answer a better one.

The story is honestly recalled, and told with great literary beauty. Augustine describes how, in her anguish, she followed him down to the sea, doing her best to hold him back. By telling her a lie, he deceived her into thinking that he would not sail until the following day, but that night he gave her the slip. As she spent the night pleading with God to keep him from going, the ship was sailing farther from the shore.

> By her floods of tears what was she begging of you, my God, but that you would not allow me to sail? Yet in your deep counsel you heard the central point of her longing, though not granting her what she then asked, namely that you would make me what she continually prayed for.

Looking back over the years and realising how deeply he had grieved her, he describes the scene with deep poignancy and literary artistry:

> The wind blew and filled our sails, and the shore was lost to our sight. There, when morning came, she was crazed with grief. . . . But you paid no heed to her cries . . . you were to use my absence as a means of bringing her joy.

Her son was not only indifferent to her tears but dishonest. In her intense sadness, Monica continued to plead for him:

> And yet after accusing me of deception and cruelty, she turned again to pray for me and to go back to her usual home. Meanwhile I came to Rome.[43]

Monica later joined Augustine in Italy and had the great joy of seeing her son converted and baptised, along with his own son and his close friend and later episcopal colleague, Alypius. Her story is a salutary reminder that the prayers of parents for their unconverted children are heard in heaven and that God has more than one way of answering them.

Monica's story came to a jubilant ending. She planned to return with Augustine to North Africa. They were resting in Ostia preparing for the homeward journey when, in a vision, there came to them both a glimpse of heaven. Just over a week later, Monica died.

"When she breathed her last, the boy Adeodatus cried out in sorrow." But then:

> After the boy's tears had been checked, Evodius took up the psalter and began to chant a psalm. The entire household responded to him: "I will sing of your mercy and judgment, Lord."[44]

They rejoiced that she was with Christ, a woman of steadfast faith with her greatest prayer abundantly answered.

A Friend's Death

The manner of Monica's passing and Augustine's reaction to it contrast sharply with another experience of death that made a lasting impression. It is a reminder that the voice of God can be eloquent in the sadness of bereavement, reaching the bleak corners of troubled minds.

The story concerns an unnamed young man who was Augustine's closest friend during his time at Thagaste. They had known each other since childhood, attended the same school and played together, but in their early twenties their friendship deepened. Increasingly enthralled by his Manichaean novelties, Augustine turned his friend away from the Christian faith. Suddenly, the young man became desperately ill, and while he was unconscious, his parents had him baptised. Although the Manichees despised baptism as an item of useless ceremonial, Augustine did not concern himself too much about what had happened. He was sure that, on recovery, his friend would still be a committed Manichee. All through the illness he did not leave the bedside, but when his friend felt better, Augustine was appalled to hear him make open confession of personal faith in Christ. A sickroom was not the place for a religious argument, but Augustine wanted to be sure that his friend had not become a committed Christian:

I attempted to joke with him, imagining that he too would laugh with me about the baptism which he had received when far away in mind and sense. . . . He was horrified at me as if I were an enemy, and with amazing and immediate frankness advised me that, if I wished to be his friend, I must stop saying this kind of thing to him. . . . After a few days, while I was absent, the fever returned, and he died.

Shocked and grief-stricken, Augustine wandered around in dazed bewilderment. He recalls the experience with vivid and painful detail, only fully understood by those who have known the anguish of great loss:

Everything on which I set my gaze was death. My home town became a torture to me . . . all that I had shared with him was without him transformed into a cruel torment. My eyes looked for him everywhere, and he was not there. . . . I had become to myself a vast problem . . . weeping had replaced my friend.

God was speaking to him through his distress; possibly for the first time, Augustine realised he was afraid of death. The sad messenger of intense loss had awakened deep thoughts about his eternal destiny:

I found myself heavily weighed down by a sense of being tired of living and scared of dying. . . . Someone has well said of his friend, "he was half my soul." . . . So my life was to me a horror. . . . But when my weeping stopped, my soul felt burdened by a vast load of misery.

Augustine's Manichaean beliefs were of no help to him. He later wished that there and then he had cried to God: "I should have lifted myself to you, Lord, to find a cure. I knew that, but did not wish it or have the strength for it."

In his anguish Augustine felt that "the lost life of those who die becomes the death of those still living." Though unbearably painful, the bereavement marked an important stage in his spiritual odyssey. Even in loss there were things to gain. The death evaluated for him the immense treasure of good friendship. It confronted him with the lucid, firm assurance of a young friend who, through trouble, had been brought to clear faith in Christ and peace with God. It showed him that, in the most sorrowful experience of his life thus far, a futile religion had left him without hope. It caused him to think seriously about death. It warned him of the transitoriness of life:

> The reason why that grief had penetrated me so easily and deeply was that I had poured out my soul onto the sand by loving a person sure to die as if he would never die.[45]

But all is not lost if a bewildered seeker perceives that this life is not everything.

A Teacher's Failure

One of the many impressive features about the *Confessions* is the way Augustine's story becomes a vehicle for the exposition of great theological truths. The unusually long narrative about the death of his friend presents a number of pastoral reflections on bereavement, but it also conveys a firm doctrinal certainty; a sovereign God can use life's costly experiences to communicate great truths to us. Augustine finds several opportunities to remind us that we do not always know what God is doing when he allows us to suffer adversity. This theme of "not knowing" is a characteristic feature in the unfolding story. Augustine cannot imagine why he has been robbed of a close friend. Monica weeps, not knowing why God ignores her prayer.

When, because of his bereavement, Augustine left Thagaste for Carthage, he was in for another disappointment, but a hidden God was silently at work in it all. By this time he had been a Manichaean "hearer" for several years, and in the course of his reading and thinking, a number of perplexing questions had occupied his mind. He found several things about the teaching of the Manichees difficult to relate to other theories about life and truth. He had longed for years to be in the company of a gifted Manichaean scholar so that he could "bounce off" his problems.

Suddenly, to his great joy, he heard that one of their leaders, Faustus, was coming to Carthage. Nobody was better suited to the task. This Manichaean bishop was one of their most outstanding thinkers and speakers. Over the years he had written forcefully against the authority of the Bible. With the Old Testament's emphasis on degrading ceremonial such as animal sacrifice and its stories of people with questionable morals, how could Christians respect its message? As for the New Testament, it might be good in parts, but only the Holy Spirit could show us what was authentic, and he had revealed all that to Mani and his successors. Augustine eagerly anticipated his conversations with Faustus. As a young man, he had "admired his soft eloquence," knowing that many had been "captured as a result of his smooth talk."

When Faustus arrived at Carthage (around 382), Augustine was in his late twenties, needing something more than silky words. He was in pursuit of truth and "was interested not in the decoration of the vessel in which his discourse was served up but in the knowledge put before me to eat by this Faustus, held in high respect among the Manichees."

Augustine had taken the trouble to prepare thoroughly for his first meeting with the teacher, contrasting the discoveries of gifted philosophers (particularly on natural science) with "the lengthy fables of the Manichees." For example, the philosophers of his day could skillfully predict the "eclipses of sun and moon, foretelling the day, the hour, and whether total or partial."

Although many of these philosophers were vain and conceited, God had given them these insights into truth, and Augustine was eager to learn from them. They do not know (here is the theme again) how deeply they are indebted to God, but they are certainly being used by him. Armed with the fruit of their studies, Augustine confronted the famous teacher with his urgent questions. He particularly wanted to know how Faustus related these scientific discoveries, about astronomy for example, to the weird stories by which the Manichees explained such phenomena. They interpreted eclipses as fierce conflicts between light and darkness during which the sun and moon turn their eyes away so as not to look. Augustine wanted to know why Mani and his successors sought to delve into "solstices and equinoxes or eclipses of luminaries" in the first place. A Christian believer might be totally ignorant of such things but firm in faith; he can love God "whom all things serve" (including sun, moon, stars) even though "he may know nothing about the circuits of the Great Bear."

Augustine was bitterly disappointed at the teacher's response. The man offered no help at all. Nine years of Manichaean instruction had got Augustine's "vagabond mind" nowhere. Whenever he had shared his honest perplexities with other Manichees, they had assured him that Faustus would deal with all his doubts. In fact, Faustus offered no more than any other Manichee; the only difference was that he phrased it with more polish: "But what could the most presentable waiter do for my thirst by offering precious cups? . . . Fine style does not make something true."

In opportunities for public discussion with Faustus, Augustine was not allowed to put his questions. When he met the teacher privately, he was shocked to discover how ignorant the man was. Outside the literature of the Manichees he was not remotely well-read. Augustine was the first to concede that genuine belief in God did not depend on having a wide knowledge of astronomy. But in the Manichaean system, questions of astronomy were of great importance, and ignorance of such matters on the part of a Manichee was inexcusable. Faustus said that he did not understand the issues Augustine wished to discuss and at least had the honesty to confess it. Augustine liked the man himself well enough, and was pleased to spend time with him while he was in Carthage. However,

... the renowned Faustus ... without his will or knowledge [there is the "not knowing" theme again] had begun to loosen the bond by which I had been captured. For in your hidden providence your hands, my God, did not forsake my soul ... and you dealt with me in wonderful ways.[46]

Augustine decided to leave Carthage and go to Rome. Although at the time he did not know it, God had used the encounter with Faustus to bring him away from the useless quest he had pursued through Manichaeism for nine crucial years. God closes doors but opens others. To get Augustine to Italy, he used not only the failure of Faustus but even the behaviour of students. In Carthage it was not easy to teach because the students were ill-mannered and disruptive in lectures and behaved like mindless vandals as they roamed the streets. But God was still working in Augustine's unhappy mind. Once more we have encountered the "not knowing" sequence. Augustine does not fully understand why he yearns to get to Italy, but God knows and in his "profoundly mysterious providence" is gradually unfolding an all-wise plan:

You were at work in persuading me to go to Rome. . . . You applied the pricks which made me tear myself away from Carthage ... you knew, God, why I left Carthage and went to Rome.[47]

Leaving his distracted mother, a futile Manichaean teacher and the unruly students, Augustine boarded a ship and left by night for Italy, but the wind of God was in those sails. Those who long for spiritual maturity soon discover that there may be more to learn from life's disappointments than from its abundant joys. Once in Rome, Augustine was happy enough, but even there the academic scene was not what he expected. He found he had simply exchanged one type of student for another; at Carthage they were insolent, in Rome dishonest. It was customary in those days to pay a lecturer as the course drew to its close, and Augustine was shocked to discover that, after he had given his best in teaching, his students slunk off without paying.

Moreover, he was not only denied his income but robbed of good health as well. Even at Rome, Augustine continued his contacts with the Manichees, and they used their influence to get him a change of job, this time in Milan. They did not know it, nor did Augustine, but they had helped him to meet a man whose ministry would revolutionise his life.

A Preacher's Gifts

For ten years before Augustine's arrival in northern Italy, Ambrose had served as bishop in Milan. He had not sought the job, and over the years he had coped with considerable persecution from professing Christians not prepared to acknowledge the deity of Christ. The harsh circumstances had served to enhance rather than diminish his work, and, by the time Augustine arrived in the city, his spiritual influence was widely appreciated. Augustine makes no secret of his unpayable debt. Looking back, his dominant thought about Milan was not his promotion to a superior position as a leading orator but his meeting with a gifted preacher: "And so I came to Milan to Ambrose the bishop."

Here, once again, we meet the "not knowing" feature in Augustine's narrative. His Manichaean friends had nominated him for the post, though in doing so they severed his last link with their teaching: "My move there was to end an association with them, but neither of us knew that." He knew he was meeting Ambrose, but he did not know how significant the encounter was to be. In all these things, a sovereign God was guiding his life: "I was led to him by you, unaware that through him in full awareness, I might be led to you."

Three characteristics of Ambrose's ministry impressed Augustine as he searched for the truth. They continue to be of primary importance in the service of Christ: the integrity of his life, the quality of his work and the authority of his message. We mention them in this order because Augustine does so, but they are inseparable. When any one of the three is missing, a ministry is less than God intends it to be. Who we are, how we serve and what we share are of equal importance.

Augustine makes it clear that the character of Ambrose made the initial impact. Here was a man who did not simply talk about love, but practised it in everyday pastoral ministry. A stranger to Milan, Augustine was taken aback when Ambrose showed such obvious interest in him as a person, treating him like a son. Ambrose was a preacher not enamoured by the crowds but concerned for the individual:

> That man of God (2 Kings 1:9) received me like a father and expressed pleasure at my coming with a kindness most fitting in a bishop. I began to like him, at first indeed not as a teacher of the truth, for I had absolutely no confidence in your Church, but as a human being who was kind to me.

What we are may preach as loudly as what we say.

Augustine's second impression concerned the quality of the preacher's work; he did it well. That was sure to attract Augustine because the older Ambrose was doing the same kind of work as himself, dealing with well-chosen words and considering the dramatic impact of carefully framed sentences, the structure of an argument, the logic of what was being presented, the use of appropriate illustrations and the like. At first Augustine was not interested in the content of the preacher's message; his overwhelming disillusionment with Manichaeism momentarily robbed him of any immediate interest in spiritual things. For nine impressionable years he had been led along a false trail; he had every reason to be cautious before changing from one religion to another. Augustine had heard a lot about this preacher's art, and that is what drew him initially to the church in Milan. Had the ministry of Ambrose been careless, slovenly or indifferent, Augustine might never have crossed the threshold. Before he became a Christian, he enjoyed the services, or at least Ambrose's part in them:

I used enthusiastically to listen to him preaching to the people, not with the intention which I ought to have had, but as if testing out his oratorical skill to see whether it merited the reputation it enjoyed. . . . I hung on his diction in rapt attention, but remained bored and contemptuous of the subject matter. My pleasure was in the charm of his language. . . . Nevertheless, gradually, *though I did not realize it,* I was drawing closer.[48]

Ambrose was not content merely to preach; he did everything within his power to preach well and used every possible device to make the truth not only intelligible but attractive and memorable as well.

In time, Augustine's interest passed beyond the vehicle of the message to the message itself. He listened eagerly to Ambrose though he was "not interested in learning what he was talking about" and had even "lost any hope that a way to [God] might lie open for man." But God was working in that bewildered mind, for Augustine recalls:

Nevertheless together with the words which I was enjoying, the subject matter, in which I was unconcerned, came to make an entry into my mind. I could not separate them. While I opened my heart in noting the eloquence with which he spoke, there also entered no less the truth which he affirmed.

It all took time. As the light began to break through, he saw the weakness of Manichaeism and came to realise that most of its criticism of biblical Christianity was unfounded. Hovering in a void, he could not fully accept the Christian message but no longer felt free to attack it. At that stage he neither abandoned the Manichees nor identified fully with the Christians, even thinking there might "be an equally valid defence for both." Gradually, the unscientific Manichaean speculations about "the physical world and all the natural order," their bizarre teaching about sun, moon and stars, began to edge him away from his nine-year allegiance.

As the weeks went by, he found himself contrasting the incompetence of Faustus at Carthage with the persuasive excellence of Ambrose in Milan. During one period he doubted everything, but in time, though only as a genuine enquirer, he enrolled as a catechumen in the church at Milan. He was willing to learn what the Christian message was really all about until, as he put it, "some clear light should come by which I could direct my course."[49] That light was in the Bible, expounded publicly by Ambrose and studied privately by Augustine.

Augustine had serious intellectual problems about the Christian faith, notably concerning the nature of God, the origin of evil and the authority of Scripture. He desperately wanted to talk such matters over with the great preacher, but the bishop seemed so engrossed in innumerable pastoral interviews at Milan that Augustine did not feel it right to burden him with anything else. Ambrose had brought him a long way, but for him to come to faith, God used a voice from the past as well as a messenger in the present.

A Scholar's Testimony

Augustine reflected on his long search for truth: "And here I was already thirty, and still mucking about in the same mire in a state of indecision, avid to enjoy present fugitive delights."[50]

He read avidly, not simply the New Testament but perhaps even more the literature of ancient and contemporary philosophy, struggling to find intellectual satisfaction and the answers to life's pressing questions. Some of the Greek philosophy he read had been translated into Latin by a man named Victorinus. Imagine Augustine's delight when one day a Christian leader told him that this same Victorinus had, later in life, become a firmly committed Christian. His philosophical studies had taken him so far along the road to truth, but not far enough, and in Christ he had found the answer to his deepest needs. Augustine was told how Victorinus had been brought to personal faith and with what exuberant joy the Christians in Rome had witnessed his baptism.

Naturally Augustine wanted to know by what means a pagan idolater with such a brilliant mind had become convinced about Christ and his gospel. How did God make an opening in that kind of heart? He was told that "Victorinus read holy Scripture, and all the Christian books he investigated with special care."

Simplicianus, the friend who shared this testimony with Augustine, had known Victorinus personally and had been instrumental in leading the gifted man to public commitment. The great scholar had been more than willing to believe but to make public profession of his faith was costly for one of Rome's leading orators: "He was afraid to offend his friends, proud devil-worshippers." But, after reading the Scripture, and especially the searching word of Christ about denying him before men, he "drank in courage" and gave in his name for baptism.

Simplicianus told Augustine that in Rome it was the church's practice to encourage new converts to make their profession of faith "which is expressed in set form" from "an elevated place." However, the church's leaders recognised that, for a variety of reasons, some believers might find that difficult, so timid people were permitted to declare the creed privately. The leaders thoughtfully offered Victorinus the opportunity of a private affirmation, but he would have none of it. He told them that as a city orator, all his main work had been public, so he had no intention now of becoming secretive about the greatest discovery of his life: "How much less should he be afraid of proclaiming your word, when he used to feel no fear in using his own words before crowds of frenzied pagans."

Augustine listened intently as Simplicianus told him about the day the great man made his confession, the stillness of the crowd as he mounted the steps, the astonishment and the "murmur of delighted talk as all the people who knew him spoke his name one to another." His well-known name was mouthed by the people, overjoyed that such a man had been won for Christ: "All of them wanted to clasp him to their hearts, and the hands with which they embraced him were their love and their joy."

The telling of such a moving story was all that Augustine needed. A believer's costly experience from the past had spoken as powerfully as the preaching of Ambrose in the present. By shedding his secrecy, Victorinus had no idea how influential his witness would be. Whenever we claim the strength to do anything for Christ, we never know how effective it may become or how long its fruit may remain. For Augustine a brave man's testimony from former days was calling him to the same commitment: "As soon as your servant Simplicianus told me this story about Victorinus, I was ardent to follow his example."[51]

Augustine scarcely had time to recover from its impact before another believer, Ponticianus, visited his home, and God used him to relate the experience of another Christian, Antony of Egypt. This story contained a similar message of commitment and trust, and Augustine learned how influential a written account of Antony's story had been in the life of Ponticianus and his friends.

The visitor thought he was simply relating a personal story, but, on top of everything else, God was using it dramatically in Augustine's life to make him see himself as he really was:

> But while he was speaking, Lord, you turned my attention back to myself. You took me up from behind my own back where I had placed myself because I did not wish to observe myself. . . . I looked and was appalled, but there was no way of escaping from myself. If I tried to avert my gaze from myself, his story continued relentlessly, and you once again placed me in front of myself; you thrust me before my own eyes so that I should discover my iniquity and hate it.[52]

The penetrating story of Antony's commitment had made him look squarely into his own face, and he did not like what he saw. It was not only spiritually enlightening but morally disturbing. It said things about his personal lifestyle and ethical values that he found difficult to take, but the disruption was a vital element in his spiritual pilgrimage. It brought him to the verge of that garden in Milan and the moment of grateful discovery. Those who want God in their lives must be ready to see themselves, their past failure, their present sin and their future danger. As Augustine read Paul's words in the garden, he discovered with joy that he need not linger over the dirty garments of his own life. Christ was giving him a better robe: "Put on the Lord Jesus Christ and make no provision for the flesh" (Rom 13:14).

The miracle had begun. One of the world's most outstanding Christians was entering the kingdom. He had not pursued the quest alone, and it was not long before others joined him. His friends, Alypius and Nebridius, equally concerned to know Christ, were just as clearly won. It was the close of the struggle but only the beginning of a fight. Augustine's ministry in an African seaport was to span the world. Well beyond his lifetime his extensive writings were to be read and studied by people in continents and cultures of which he knew nothing. When men and women surrender their lives to Christ, a work begins that lasts for eternity.

MARTIN LUTHER

A Simple Way to Pray

Let Prayer
Be the First Business

Augustine's *Confessions* exercised a profound influence on the development of Christian spirituality and was treasured in monastic houses throughout Europe for a thousand years. His convictions formed the basis of a carefully structured medieval theology developed by Thomas Aquinas in his voluminous *Summa Theologica*, compulsory reading for church leaders throughout the Middle Ages.

Such works were part of the daily theological diet of a young German monk whose impact on the story of world Christendom was to become as momentous as his great theological mentor, Augustine of Hippo.

Martin Luther was born at Eisleben in 1483, the son of a German miner, Hans Luther. Directly against his father's wishes, young Luther entered an Augustinian house at Erfurt in 1505. Even then, in his early twenties, he was troubled about his eternal security. He joined the Hermits of St Augustine to honour a vow made during a thunderstorm. Terrified at the prospect of unprepared death, he had cried out, in terms typical of medieval piety, "St Anne, help me, and I will become a monk."

A sincere and devoted novice, Luther proved to be also a highly gifted student. In 1508 he was called to the chair of moral philosophy in the new University of Wittenberg, and after further study began, in 1509, to lecture on the Bible as well. In 1512 he received a licence to become a candidate for a doctorate and was made professor of Holy Scripture.

Next to the teaching of the Bible, nothing was more formative in Luther's theology and experience than the writings of Augustine. In his early thirties, Luther came into a saving experience of Christ, deeply assured that, in Paul's language, he was "justified by faith," made "right with God" not by any merits of his own, or of the saints, but solely through the generous, undeserved act of a supremely merciful God.

Luther was deeply disturbed that thousands of his own countrymen were deceived by the erroneous teaching of indulgence sellers like John Tetzel. Indulgences were originally remissions of penance imposed by the church on those who had confessed and repented of sin. In time, indulgences came to be sold for money, and the system took on the character of a commercial transaction. Official doctrine still insisted on the need for penitence and denied that remission of sin could be obtained by buying indulgences. But by 1517 most people had come to believe that the purchase of an indulgence guaranteed remission of guilt as well as of the penalty.

Luther challenged his contemporaries to a serious debate on these crucial issues by posting his Ninety-five Theses to the door of the Castle Church at Wittenberg. Though the date of that event— All Saints' Eve, October 31, 1517—has become world-famous, at the time there was nothing remotely unusual in such an action; it was a common way of inviting academic colleagues to an informed theological discussion. The formal debate never took place, but the issues Luther raised have continued to divide Catholics from Protestants, as non-Catholics came to be known. Within a few years, a papal pronouncement declared Luther a heretic, and hope of reconciliation had gone.

In the years that followed, Luther continued to lecture in theology at Wittenberg and shared with others in the shaping of Protestant church life in Germany and beyond. Throughout his eventful life, Luther was, like Augustine, a pastor as well as a theological teacher and author. His extensive writings (he produced something every few weeks) were easily distributed by means of the recently acquired art of printing and quickly spread all over Europe. Throughout these years, Luther also cared for the spiritual life of a local congregation, helping to see his people through dark and difficult times. All his writings (often printed without his permission, and certainly without financial gain for him) constantly reflect this deep pastoral concern.

When, for example, the plague—the terrifying Black Death— reached Wittenberg, the local university moved to Jena, but Luther insisted on remaining in the town. He made his own home into a local hospital and, in the midst of this appalling scourge, wrote *Whether One May Flee from a Deadly Plague*. The heart of the book shares the conviction that in normal circumstances, it is only sensible for families to move to a place of safety, but that does not mean everybody must leave. The more demanding question for a Christian is not whether it is wise to flee from the plague, but whether it is right to forsake our neighbour who may be in desperate need of physical and spiritual help.

Similarly, but less dramatically, other pastoral writings reveal a man eager to help his congregation through the everyday traumas of sixteenth-century life, such as depression, sickness, bereavement and persecution. His brief statement written to help distressed women who had suffered a miscarriage is a model of compassionate sensitivity and pastoral artistry. A happily married man with children, he too had suffered the loss of a child; he had also experienced ill-health and knew the extreme pain of losing close friends, martyred for their faith. Inevitably, the writings of such a man throb with tenderness and practical care.

Luther continued this caring pastoral ministry to the closing days of his life. Two noblemen from his home territory became bitterly estranged, and Luther knew that such quarrels could have serious repercussions for innocent people who lived on their lands. What began as a personal grievance could easily spread into a calamitous local feud. Although extremely ill, Luther travelled to Eisleben in ghastly winter conditions, determined to do his utmost to reconcile the opposing counts. The letters he sent home give some indication of the intense animosity between the two men, "embittering each other with letters," and of Luther's painful struggle to effect a satisfactory peace.

Eventually, the counts were reconciled, and on the following day (14 February 1546), with his mission accomplished, Luther died. Like Bunyan in the following century, his closing hours were spent on an errand of mercy in an attempt to bring to an end the enmity between two alienated people. Christians must not love in word only, but in deed and in truth. His pastoral care was a necessary practical expression of his reconciling gospel and, having loved his own, he too must love them to the end.

Throughout life, the Reformer had innumerable pastoral opportunities and often used his pen in responding to specific requests for counsel. One day in the mid-1530s, Luther's barber, Peter Beskendorf, asked his minister for some practical advice about prayer. Luther had known "the master barber" for many years and was eager to help; typically, he wrote a little book specially for Beskendorf. This short thirty-four-page manual, *A Simple Way to Pray, for a Good Friend,* first published in the spring of 1535, went into four editions in its first year. It soon made its way into Christian homes all over Europe, and over the intervening centuries has been widely recognised as a classic among the devotional writings of Lutherans. It illustrates Luther's devotion as a pastor and is a fine example of his gifts as a highly effective communicator in the sixteenth century.

Peter Beskendorf must have been grateful when Luther first placed it in his hands; but within a short while, he was to be in greater need of its clear message of forgiveness and its reiterated plea for courageous, holy living. Luther's barber encountered hard times. A quick-tempered man, Beskendorf was irritated by his son-in-law's persistent bragging. Dietrich had served in the army and wearisomely paraded his skills in self-defence, asserting that he could so flex his stomach muscles that if he were attacked with a dagger it would be impossible to hurt him. One Easter Saturday evening he dared somebody to attempt it, and his father-in-law took up the challenge. Beskendorf probably had too much to drink that night; the dagger penetrated his son-in-law's stomach, and within hours he was dead.

Luther and others pleaded for the offender, and, given the unusual circumstances, Beskendorf was spared capital punishment; but he was exiled from home and forced to live in Dessau for the rest of his life. This buoyant man's life changed overnight. Emphasising the severe restriction of enforced exile, Luther's friend Philip Melanchthon said that Beskendorf, broken and impoverished, was left with nothing but his head, "that part of himself which he can stick out of the window." A refugee in a strange city, he had lost everything; home, family, possessions had all gone. In the dark days of his later life he must have derived immense comfort from this appealing little booklet written especially for him, about the nature and value of prayer. It is of special interest because it does not claim to be a formal theology of prayer but a delightful personal account of the Reformer's own practice of daily prayer: "Dear Master Peter: I give you the best I have; I tell you how I myself pray. May our Lord grant you and everyone to do better. Amen."

In sharing his experience Luther explores a variety of themes that are of continuing importance for every Christian.

THE CHALLENGE OF PRAYER

Luther begins by putting his reader at ease, recognising that prayer is not always easy. He identifies four difficulties about prayer: disinclination, procrastination, limitation and opposition.

The first problem is disinclination; we may not always want to pray. Luther freely admits to his friend Peter that he has not always felt like praying: "First, whenever I feel that I have grown cold and disinclined to pray . . . I take my little Psalter, hasten into my room. . . ."

There are times when the pressures of life are such that,

although we know that we are better people if we pray, the sheer weight of anxiety or preoccupation with other things diverts us from prayer. Luther knew that experience only too well. He was nothing if not honest. Once, when threatened by the Catholic authorities, he had been compassionately "kidnapped" by the sympathetic Elector of Saxony and given protective asylum in the Wartburg Castle. Forcefully isolated from his work at Wittenberg, Luther became unwell, describing this bleak experience as his "isle of Patmos," "my wilderness." During that time he found it almost impossible to pray and wrote to his friend Melanchthon, saying:

> I sit here like a fool and, hardened in leisure, pray little. . . . I do not know whether God has turned away from me. . . . Already eight days have passed in which I have written nothing, in which I have not prayed or studied; this is partly because of temptations of the flesh, partly because I am tortured by other burdens.[1]

Luther knew there could be times in the life of Peter the barber when prayer might not be easy, and he wanted to prepare him for such experiences. We must pray whether we feel like it or not. Prayer must never be at the mercy of our vacillating moods and highly changeable emotions.

A more likely problem is procrastination. We freely acknowledge the importance of prayer and know that we will be better for it, but other things need to be done, and prayer is not an urgent priority. We will certainly pray—but not yet. Luther tells Beskendorf that it is essential to fix a set time for prayer and keep that daily appointment with God whatever else happens: "Therefore, it is a good thing to let prayer be the first business of the morning and the last of the evening."

If this vital daily discipline is neglected, prayer will become a dispensable option, constantly neglected in favour of more pressing duties or assignments. In a busy life Luther knew the danger only too well:

Guard yourself carefully against such false and deceitful thoughts that keep whispering: "Wait awhile. In an hour or so I will pray. I must first finish this or that." Thinking such thoughts, we get away from prayer into business that will hold us and involve us till the prayer of the day comes to naught.

Luther identifies another problem that is not frequently mentioned in books about prayer. It is the danger of limitation, of restricting prayer solely to the words we speak in the presence of God. Luther does not minimise the crucial nature of Christian prayer as communion with God, but asserts that we can pray by what we *do* as well as by what we say. Sometimes other things may be more important than prayer, "especially if necessity demands them."

We must remember that he writes all this against the background of monastic piety, elevated throughout the Middle Ages as the highest spiritual ideal. Nothing was considered more holy than retreating into some isolated monastic house to devote oneself to prayer and worship. Here Luther asserts that it "may very well be that there are some works which are as good or better than prayer."

A time may come when the Lord wants us to do a specific thing for him and not simply talk to him about what might be done. For example, if a member of our family, a friend or a neighbour is unwell, it is natural to give ourselves to earnest prayer for the sick person's recovery; but God expects us to do something more than pray. As if to give added weight to what he has said, Luther quotes an early Christian scholar who lived in a monastic community in late fourth-century Bethlehem—Jerome, a contemporary of Augustine. Of all people, he would not say anything to marginalise the ministry of prayer, and Luther repeats Jerome's saying, "*All* the work of believers is prayer." He also mentions a familiar proverb of his day: "He who works faithfully prays twice."

Yet, given this truth, Luther identifies a danger. An unspiritual man or woman might make this a cloak for prayerlessness: "I prefer to do practical things and leave the praying to others." So, while Luther insists that, given the right attitude, motivation and circumstances, some good works can be truly prayerful, he is anxious to protect his readers from the idea that prayer is secondary to works and that if they do good deeds toward their neighbours, or perform the works of religion, then it does not matter whether they pray or not. He insists:

> We must be careful not to be weaned away from true prayer and finally come to interpret prayer to mean all kinds of works which are necessary but not true prayer after all, and thus in the end become careless, lazy, cold and bored with prayer itself.

Luther exposes a further problem about prayer—opposition. He knows that when we do not pray, someone leaps with joyous delight—the devil. In this little book on prayer, Luther frequently refers to the persistent and malevolent work of the enemy of souls. The Reformer is in no doubt whatever about either the devil's existence or his persistence. We may become indolent about our Christian privileges and responsibilities in prayer, but the devil is never idle in preventing our prayers: "For the devil who besets us is not lazy or careless, and our flesh is still all too active and eager to sin and inclined to be contrary to the spirit of prayer."

There was a special reason why Luther drew attention to the work of the devil in this little book. Once, when he went into the barber's shop for a haircut, Peter Beskendorf told him that he was planning to write a book. Luther expressed interest in the idea until Beskendorf told him it would be a book warning people about the power and deceitfulness of the devil. Luther teased him that a project of that kind had its dangers; the adversary does not like to have his works exposed in writing. Some days later Luther sent Peter some playful verses:

> *So brash and bold the devil is*
> *Full of knavery, trick and guile*
> *That Master Peter had better look sharp*

Lest he try to trick the devil
And it backfires upon himself . . .

So Luther begins his book on prayer on the note of sombre realism: Prayer may not always be an attractive proposition. The devil does his utmost so to manipulate the desires of the flesh that we become increasingly independent of God and imperceptibly drift away from our spiritual moorings. Then prayer will no longer be a priority. Yet, skillful pastor that he is, Luther is not content to emphasise negative things for long; he quickly moves on to explain how the prayer of a believer can be enriched.

THE PURPOSE OF PRAYER

He begins with our approach to prayer and considers how best we can prepare ourselves for it. Luther emphasises that prayer is more than asking. Prayer is life's greatest reminder of the reality of God. It is simply being in the presence of God so that we can absorb a renewed sense of his greatness and our constant need of him.

Luther is firmly persuaded that Christians pray best with an open Bible in front of them. He believes that good prayer is responsive; it is speaking back to the God who has already addressed us in Scripture. It is for this reason that meditation is important for Luther. It is the spiritual exercise whereby we listen intently to what God is saying to us through a biblical passage and allow it deeply to permeate our hearts and minds, reverently pondering its message, constantly and gratefully repeating its words so that as it becomes part of our mental framework, we are inspired to pray.

Luther suggests that we begin our prayers by reciting some part of Scripture quietly to ourselves. As we meditate unhurriedly on its message, it produces in us reverence, gratitude and expectancy for the experience of prayer, so that we guard against rushing into the presence of God, babbling familiar words and reciting our urgent requests. Meditation will impress upon us the thought that God may well be wanting to say something to us, which transcends anything we may say to him. In sharing his own practice of prayer, Luther says that he goes to his room,

> or if it is during the day and I have time, to the church where others are gathered, and begin to say the Ten Commandments, the Creed, and then, if I have time, some words of Christ, Paul or the Psalms, saying them quietly to myself just as children do.

We shall soon have occasion to see that disciplined, structured meditation on these great passages forms the basis of Luther's own prayer life, but at this stage it is enough to note that this is how he began his prayers—patiently listening to God as he has revealed himself to us in his word. His choice of passages is illuminating—initially the Ten Commandments and then the Creed.

The commandments are not simply a series of divine rules people are to obey. They reveal the nature of God. They do not begin by announcing what we are to do but by declaring what God is like and what he has done: "I am the Lord who brought you out of Egypt, out of the land of slavery" (Deut 5:6).

By quietly reciting the commandments at the beginning of his prayer time, Luther reminds himself of four great truths they enshrine for us: who God is, what he has done, who we are and what he wants us to be.

The commandments begin by asserting something about God. They are not cold, legalistic instructions, but a sensitive revelation of the nature and character of the God who is speaking to his people. "I am the Lord" recalls the name by which he revealed himself to Moses at the burning bush. When Moses was told of the forthcoming deliverance, he naturally asked what he was to say when the enslaved Israelites asked for the name of the God who had spoken. God answered: "This is what you are to say to the Israelites: 'I AM has sent me to you'" (Ex 3:13-14). He is the ever-present, never-failing, all-powerful God.

Therefore, when Luther encourages his contemporaries to begin their prayers reverently by recalling the commandments, he invites them to consider the God they are addressing. He is a sovereign God who controls their destiny; and not just the destiny of the fearful Moses and the despondent Israelites, but also that of the arrogant Egyptians and of the vulnerable Luther, the conscience-stricken Beskendorf—and of you and me.

Moreover, the commandments go on to declare that this eternal, sovereign God is omnipotent. He does not simply speak to Moses but will act savingly on behalf of his people. He is the God who liberated them from Egyptian slavery. He is the only God; there are no others. Idolatry is out of the question. He is a jealous God who will not tolerate any suggestion in the Israelites' religious practice that their God is one among many, leaving them free to compromise with other religions. He is a loving God, demonstrating dependable covenant compassion to thousands who love him and keep his commandments.

He is a saving God, able to take people in the worst of life's situations and bring them out "with a mighty hand and an outstretched arm." He is a generous God who longs only for his people's good, "that it may go well" with them and that they "may live long" in the land he is to give them. He is the living God, so they must not rob anybody of a life he has given. He is a loyal God, so they are not to live otherwise in their marital relationships. He is a truthful God, so they must not speak lies against their neighbours. He is an omniscient God, seeing and knowing everything, even the secret thoughts of a covetous heart and a materialistic, grasping spirit. The tenth commandment is an eloquent reminder that here is something more than a set of rules. How can anybody detect secret covetousness but the God who sees all things?

Here then in the Decalogue is a rich portrait of God, who he is and what he does—revelation and redemption. That is at the heart of the commandments, and God's demand is simply this—that his people should be like him. If he values life, so must they. If he is reliable and trustworthy in relationships, how can they possibly be anything else? If he is holy, then they too must be pure in every aspect of their behaviour.

Furthermore, Luther quietly recited the commandments because they are not only a revelation of God but also an exposure of ourselves. Here we see the kind of people we are always in danger of being and becoming, but for the grace of God—idolatrous, ungrateful, irreverent, forgetful, indifferent to the working conditions of other people, disrespectful to parents, aggressive and violent towards those we dislike, unfaithful in life's most intimate relationships, greedy, lustful for things that belong to other people, ready to say things that are blatantly untrue even though others may suffer because of it and always wanting just a little more than we have.

It is for this reason that the English Puritans, as well as Luther and Calvin, frequently described God's law in the commandments as a looking-glass or mirror, designed by God to show us ourselves as we really are and not as we might vainly imagine ourselves to be. When Luther was expounding Galatians he stated this very clearly:

> The proper office of the law is to show unto us our sins, to make us guilty, to humble us . . . and finally to take from us all help . . . but yet altogether to this end, that we may . . . obtain all good things.[2]

When Luther compiled his liturgy for those Reformed congregations he knew best, he wrote a metrical version of the commandments with the provision that after every verse the congregation could unite in the response: "Lord, have mercy upon us." The commandments remind us that we are sinners. Our times for believing and dependent prayer are not occasions to parade our merits or assert our moral worth. They are moments when we are reminded of our immense need, when we recall with gratitude that we come to God in prayer so that, however deep our sin, we may be gloriously forgiven.

The commandments also show us what we can be by the grace of God. These high standards are set for us by a God who has not only given us this pattern for happy and useful living but who has promised the strength to obey his word. He would not call us to something utterly impossible. Such a standard would only embarrass us; instead it is set down for us in Scripture to inspire within us the desire for a better quality of life. Moreover, the lifestyle God expects of us will affect every aspect of human existence. The commandments relate to our attitude to God, our families, neighbours, employees, even our animals, which also deserve a weekly rest day.

So when Luther told Peter Beskendorf that he might begin his prayers as he himself did, by reciting the commandments, he was making an excellent suggestion, and one that might enrich our own communion with God. It could save us from rushing into God's presence unthinkingly, irreverently, preoccupied with things we desire from him, without first thinking of what he has done for us and what he desires from us—love, worship, obedience, holiness and service.

Next, Luther says he quietly recites the Creed. In other words, in the presence of God he gratefully affirms his faith and declares his confidence in the God he is approaching. Luther has more to say about meditating on the Creed at the close of his book, but at this stage we simply note that as he begins to pray, he reflects on the greatness and glory of God in his triune nature and being, Father, Son and Holy Spirit. Here are all the unlimited resources of the eternal and ever-blessed God. Surely the God who created the world can do anything. Will not the Christ who has redeemed continue lovingly to keep his own? Has not the Holy Spirit sufficient resources to enrich the lives of all who have been entrusted to his ministry of instruction, conviction, companionship and power? These are the thoughts that fill Luther's mind long before he ventures to ask for anything.

THE ESSENCE OF PRAYER

Luther says that once the heart has prepared itself in the way he has suggested, the praying man or woman needs to speak personally with God and not simply recite well-worn words that have been written by others. But he wants to give his barber all the help he can, and so, without providing him with a set of written prayers, he shares an example of how he begins to pray:

> Now when the heart has been warmed by this recitation of the Ten Commandments, the Creed, etc., and it comes to itself, then kneel down or stand with folded hands and eyes lifted to heaven, and say or think as briefly as you can:
>
> Heavenly Father, dear God, I am a poor, unworthy sinner, not worthy to lift up my eyes or hands to pray to thee. But since thou hast commanded us all to pray and promised to hear us, and through thy dear Son, our Lord Jesus Christ also hast taught us how to pray, I come in obedience to this command. I come relying on thy gracious promise, I pray in the name of my Lord Jesus Christ with all thy holy Christians on earth, as he has taught us: "Our Father, who art in heaven," etc. Pray this (the Lord's Prayer) through, word for word. Then repeat a part or as much as you wish.

This example of an introductory prayer is a choice model. Within the limited compass of a few brief sentences, the Reformer has compressed a wealth of rich doctrinal convictions: the fatherhood of God, the fact of sin, the necessity of personal confession, the teaching of Christ, the importance of obedience and dependence, the promise of grace, the power of Christ's unique name and the supportive fellowship of believing people everywhere.

Luther wants his friend to realise that whenever he prays, he declares his confidence in the great unchanging realities of Christian faith and experience. Some Christian prayer is in danger of failing miserably at this very level. It can be painfully subjective, constantly dependent on the fluctuating changes of a person's emotional barometer. As he prays, Luther wants to be controlled not by his variable feelings but by the objective truths of Christian doctrine. He may change, and his circumstances may vary, but these things remain, and he keeps them uppermost in his mind at the place of prayer.

THE PATTERN OF PRAYER

Luther suggests that our prayers need to take the form of orderly and unhurried meditation on some great passage of Scripture, and what better than the prayer that Jesus taught his disciples. He divides the Lord's Prayer into seven sections, showing his reader how each petition within the prayer can be used imaginatively as a basis for our own prayers. In this way Luther gives his daily prayer a specific framework to ensure that he prays regularly for important things and not just about those personal, domestic, parochial or even peripheral issues that dominate his mind at the moment he prays.

Luther provides his barber friend with some examples of the kind of prayer he might offer under each heading, though he urges him not to copy his phrases, "for then in the end this would become a mere babbling of vain, empty words read from a book, as were the rosary of the laity and the prayers of priests and monks." He longs that individual prayers might become the spontaneous out-pouring of love to God and an expression of daily reliance upon him. His aim is not to provide Peter Beskendorf with a set of someone else's prayers to read but

> only to have stirred and instructed the heart as to the thoughts it should find in the Lord's Prayer. But the heart, if it is really warmed and disposed to pray, can well express these thoughts in words different from these, and no doubt, fewer words or more.

Luther makes it clear that he does not slavishly go through each of the seven sections of the Lord's Prayer, automatically reciting it as a mechanically repetitive ritual. Some days his heart and mind are so warmed to one particular aspect that he remains entirely within that section and allows its teaching to determine the form of his prayers for that day:

> Often enough it happens that I so lose myself in the rich thoughts of one part or petition that I let all the other six go.

And when such rich, good thoughts come, one should let the other prayers go and give place to these thoughts.

With this important proviso in our minds, we look now at how Luther used these seven sections of the Lord's Prayer to inspire and shape his daily conversation with God.

Honour His Uniqueness

Luther's opening prayer under the first petition, "hallowed be thy name," reflects the tense circumstances of his times. Protestant believers were a persecuted minority, and Luther's concern for the glory of God naturally causes him to reflect on those who dishonour God's name in various parts of Europe. His prayer that God will "root out and destroy the abomination, idolatry and heresy of the Turk, the pope, and all false teachers and factious spirits" may appear harsh in our age of toleration and, at times, unhelpful compromise. His use of the prayer's opening petition demonstrates that Luther's prayers are relevant, passionate and realistic.

First, his prayers are relevant, closely related to current circumstances. When he prays he does not retreat into an insular cocoon that disregards the pressures of everyday life. Rather, he presents the needs of the world in the presence of a sovereign God who rules the nations. For him, the persecution of God's people was a frightening reality. When he prays here about the sinister activities of those who "grievously mislead so many poor sinners in the world, even killing, shedding innocent blood, and persecuting," he is not using bigoted invective. Luther does not theorise about suffering; some of his colleagues had been executed for their faith. Only a few years before he wrote this book, his friend, the pastor Leonard Kaiser, had been burned alive at the stake in Bavaria. Another, George Winkler, had been murdered in Cologne.

At the time he lost these partners, Luther was ill with kidney-stone trouble, suffering excruciating pain, at times on the verge of death. The plague had reached Wittenberg, and his little boy Hans

was desperately unwell. All the forces of evil seemed to be di
against him. It was then, in 1527, that he wrote his famous hymn,
"A Safe Stronghold Our God Is Still." Its firm and strong truths are
not exaggerated poetic licence. Luther's security was in the
unchanging God:

> And though they take our life,
> Goods, honour, children, wife,
> Yet is their profit small;
> These things shall vanish all,
> The city of God remaineth.

We must bear these things in mind if we think his language about
Turk and pope a little fierce; the days were bitterly hard.

Luther prayed with his eyes on the Lord and with a heart for
the community. It is contextual praying that grapples with life in a
hostile, unbelieving world desperately in need of our prayers. We
need to ask whether our prayers are narrowly preoccupied with
our own minute existence, rather than focused on the huge maps
of the contemporary scene. Tragic national and international situations are in urgent need of loving, intelligent intercessors. Some
influential leaders of our day, whose names are constantly before
us, may not have anybody who regularly prays for them. That
should challenge all who pray.

Second, Luther's prayers express his passionate concern for the
glory of Christ. These opening reflections on the first petition reveal
the heart of a man resolutely committed to the uniqueness of
Christ. Thousands of his religious contemporaries use Christ's
name in their liturgies, but their hearts are far from him. They
"falsely bear" that saving name, either relying on their own merits
to procure salvation or trusting in the superabundant merits of the
saints, the overflow of which might, for an appropriate fee, be
transferred to their celestial investments.

If we are tempted to regard these issues as irrelevant sixteenth-
century controversies, we must remember that millions in our own

day the world over strive by various means to earn their salvation, ignoring the unique Christ. They treasure the hope that they might achieve it by their good works, moral uprightness, religious ceremonial or ecclesiastical allegiance. People in every continent are eagerly intent on saving themselves, though they might not express it that way. Luther's message is as relevant today as when he first declared it with uncompromising simplicity and certainty as

> this one solid rock which we call the doctrine of justification
> . . . that we are redeemed from sin, death, and the devil, and
> are made partakers of eternal life, not by ourselves (and cer-
> tainly not by our works . . .) but by the help of another, the
> only begotten Son of God, Jesus Christ.[3]

Third, Luther's prayers are realistic. He lives in an alien context where some people zealously maintain that there are other ways to salvation apart from Christ. His reference to the Turk is an indication of the militant thrust of Islam in the sixteenth century, but it also reminds us of the increasingly aggressive campaign of Islamic fundamentalism in the late twentieth-century world and of the increasing pluralism within Western culture. Multifaith services in various English religious contexts are evidence of a tragic departure from the uncompromising message of the New Testament where, in a first-century pluralistic environment, the apostles shared the conviction of the Lord Jesus: "No one comes to the Father except through me" (Jn 14:6). The Christian who accepts such explicit definiteness shares the conviction of the church's first evangelists, boldly declared in the presence of a hostile audience that firmly denied the uniqueness of Christ: "Salvation is found in no one else, for there is no other name under heaven given to men by which we must be saved" (Acts 4:12).

To honour God's name in late twentieth-century society is readily to acknowledge that religious pluralism is not an option, if by that we mean there are many roads to salvation. We naturally respect everyone's religious freedom, otherwise we are under the same condemnation as the murderers of Luther's friends and the more subtle religious persecutors of our own time. People must be free to adopt and express their own religious allegiance without hindrance; but that is not the same as saying that it is a matter of indifference whom we worship and that any religious road leads ultimately to heaven. Luther put it like this: "Those who don't seek God or the Lord in Christ won't find him."[4]

Luther's prayerful reflections on the hallowing of God's name express a compassionate evangelistic concern for his neighbours and contemporaries. He turns this opening petition into a cry to God that those who do not at present hallow his name may yet be won by the preaching of the gospel. He pleads with the Lord on behalf of those who do not pray for themselves: "Convert those who need still to be converted, that they with us . . . may hallow and glorify thy name both with true and pure teaching and with good and holy lives."

Luther also reminds us that whenever we pray, we need to carry on our hearts the names of specific people who have yet to find Christ and honour God in the only way that truly pleases him—by recognising his Son as the only Saviour of their lives. Luther maintained that a passion for souls was one of the distinguishing marks of a genuine Christian. However deeply we have drunk the life-giving stream of Christ, we must always be thirsty for the salvation of others.

His friend, the young nobleman Harmut von Cronberg, gave expression to his evangelistic concern by explaining the gospel in correspondence with key people. This modest beginning eventually led to courageous work as a pamphleteer. He sent one tract, *A Letter to Mendicant Orders,* to Luther for comment before passing it to the printer. In his reply Luther affirms that personal evangelism is the compulsive expression of our indebtedness to Christ:

> It is the nature of the divine word to be heartily received by a few, but to be persecuted ruthlessly by many. . . . However, this noble word naturally brings with it a burning hunger and unquenchable thirst that can never be filled. Even though

many thousands of people believed in it, we would still desire that no person should want for it. Such thirst is ever active and knows no rest, but impels us to speak.

Always realistic, Luther reminds von Cronberg that this desire to communicate the gospel is certain to be opposed:

You too have been given such a thirst for the salvation of your brethren, which is a reliable sign of a genuine faith. It is only the gall and the vinegar that still awaits you, that is, the vilification, the shame and the persecution for the sake of your thirsty speech.[5]

Those who share the message of Christ with others know that the word must not only be audible but visible. What we are will speak as eloquently as what we say. Luther reminds Beskendorf to pray that we shall ever be saved from the hypocrisy of proclaiming "true and pure teaching" that is not matched with "good and holy lives."

Serve His Kingdom

In his meditation on the petition "thy kingdom come," Luther relates Christ's words to the persecuted church of Christ in his own day. Some abuse the authority God has given them, ruthlessly "opposing thy kingdom with all the power, might, wealth and honour which thou didst give them in order to rule the world and serve thee."

The prayer reminds us that God's gifts can be frighteningly misused. Luther is grieved that some people entrusted with leadership responsibilities in church and nation do not honour God by the way they rule their people:

They plague, hinder, and trouble the little flock of thy kingdom, which is weak, despised, and few in number. They will not suffer them on earth, and think they thereby do thee a great service.

Luther pleads again for the conversion of his contemporaries, particularly those who have set their hearts on the ruthless persecution of God's people. He begs that those who refuse to be converted to Christ will at least be restrained by an all-powerful and merciful God. The context of fierce persecution is evident. Luther knew that, for the Christian, some element of suffering is inevitable, especially for a minister of Christ. Writing to his friend Wenzeslaus Link, some months after he had posted his Ninety-five Theses, he said:

> I know perfectly well that from the beginning of the world the word of Christ has been of such a kind that whoever wants to carry the gospel into the world must necessarily, like the apostles before them, renounce everything, even expect death at any and every hour.

Those who suffer follow in the steps of their Master and his first-century apostles: "By death the gospel was bought, by deaths spread abroad, by deaths safeguarded. . . . In like manner it must take many deaths to preserve it, even to restore it."[6]

Obey His Will

Again Luther is challenged by the context of suffering to intercede for those who oppose the gospel:

> Convert those who should still acknowledge thy good will, that they with us and we with them may be obedient to thy will, ready in this obedience to suffer willingly, patiently, and gladly, all evil, cross and tribulation, learning therein to know, test and experience thy good, gracious and perfect will.

As he prays that God's will may be done in his own life, he knows that it is certainly in the purpose of God that men and women should be brought to faith in Christ. Moreover, he refuses to put limits to the grace of God; he prays for those who are persecutors that, like Saul of Tarsus, they may be won for the Redeemer.

Luther continues to share his conviction that those who want to do the will of God cannot avoid the way of suffering. Adversity is not optional for the committed believer. At some point or other, a price will be paid if we are to remain true to Christ. Identification with Christ makes opposition inevitable. Luther makes that unmistakably clear to his self-sacrificing friend, von Cronberg, when he says, "Wherever Christ is, Judas, Pilate, Herod, Caiaphas and Annas will inevitably be also, so also his cross. If not, he is not the true Christ."[7]

Acknowledge His Resources

When he comes to the petition for our daily bread, Luther widens its application beyond the issues of material food and physical provision to include all life-sustaining aspects of human existence. Using this petition, he prays for those who protect others, asking that God will give "to all kings, princes and lords good counsel and the will to preserve their lands and people in peace and justice." He prays not simply for rulers but for people, that all his prince's subjects will have "grace to serve loyally and obediently," and further extends his prayer to include numerous professions, "to citizens, and farmers that they may be devout and show love and loyalty toward one another."

Luther knows the immense blessing of a godly community, and in bringing these political and social issues within the compass of daily prayer, he sets us a fine example.

In contemporary society, our friends in CARE (Christian Action, Research and Education) and other organisations concerned for national welfare provide excellent material to help us in daily intercession on behalf of our own community. They encourage us to pray intelligently for members of government and their families; to intercede with the God of peace about the alarming spread of violence in our society; to pray for the police force and leaders within our local communities, many of whom are uncertain how we can halt the rise in violent crime. They invite us to pray for those who endeavour to persuade our government and the broadcasting authorities to take appropriate action to reduce the aggressive and morally degrading content of some magazines, videos, games, films and television programmes.

We need to pray to the God of truth about the shaping of education policy and for those who work as teachers, especially as many of them have cause to help a growing number of children with serious problems of their own. We must beseech our Creator, the giver of life, concerning those intent on introducing legislation to permit euthanasia. We must intercede with our compassionate God for the thousands who are homeless in our society, and for dedicated people who are working for their relief and help. We need to beseech our caring Father about the abuse of children, about increasing sexual permissiveness, about complex matters in medical ethics that affect human life, about issues concerning abortion, and so one might go on. If Luther were living in our present culture, these would be the pressing concerns he would bring to the forefront of his daily prayers, and they ought not to be missing from ours.

Inspired by this petition in the Lord's Prayer, Luther also prays for his own family: "I commend to thee also my house and home, my wife and children; help me to guide them well, to provide for them, and rear them as befits a Christian."

He was a loving husband and good father, a family man who treasured the blessings of a Christian home. He knew that there is more to family life than finding enough money for food and allocating time for relaxation together. He believed it was vital to pray regularly for, and with, his wife, Katharina, and his dearly loved children. His petition may remind us of the importance of intercession for our partners and children. People living alone will want to pray for families they know (especially those in danger of disintegration) and be alert to opportunities that come to single Christians in today's world to be like "parents in the faith" to those who do not have the blessing of a committed Christian father or mother.

God has infinite resources to meet all these needs. The compassionate intercessor comes to him intelligently and confidently, believing that the multiplicity of society's needs can be fully met by an omnipotent and generous God.

Receive His Cleansing

With the fifth petition, "forgive us our trespasses," Luther concentrates on the need for personal forgiveness and the importance of maintaining a forgiving spirit towards anyone who may have hurt us. He confesses the sin of ingratitude for all God's "unspeakable benefits, both spiritual and physical." He also mentions our need of forgiveness for those times when we sin and are unaware that we grieve God: "Forgive my hidden faults" (Ps 19:12). Emphasising that forgiveness cannot be bought, earned, merited or deserved, he asks that our merciful God will not look either "upon our goodness or our wickedness" but only upon his "boundless mercy given in Christ."

Luther knows, moreover, how vital it is for our spiritual development that we do not harbour bad feelings against anybody, no matter how cruel they may have been towards us:

> Forgive also our enemies and all who do us injury or injustice, as we too forgive them from our hearts; for they hurt themselves most by provoking thee to anger and we are not helped by their destruction, but would rather see them saved with us.

With alert pastoral sensitivity, Luther knows that people who have been hurt by the sins of others may find it impossible to forgive them. In this case he urges those who cannot forgive to pray for grace, that by a miracle of God's overflowing love they may yet be able to pardon those who have offended them or damaged their lives in any way. He also inserts a note here for those who expound God's word, reminding them that this thorny issue of forgiving those who sin against us "is a matter for preaching."

Claim His Power

Under the petition "lead us not into temptation," Luther returns to the praying believer's arch-enemy, the devil. Meditating on these words, he says that "the grim devil," intent on deflecting Christians from wholehearted commitment, uses three specific devices. First, he encourages sluggish self-satisfaction, making us feel "as though we now had everything." Secondly, he steals from us our most precious possession, God's "dear Word" and then, thirdly, endeavours to "sow discord and factions" among believers.

Luther knows that the devil can only be resisted by diligent attention to the word and constant reliance on the Holy Spirit. In this artless prayer he skillfully sets the energising work of the Spirit in direct opposition to the activities of the enemy. Christians who wish to frustrate the activity of the devil in their lives pray with Luther that they will be kept "steady and alert, ardent and diligent in thy Word and service" so that they will not become "satisfied, lazy and indolent."

He says that one of the worst things for Christians is for them to imagine that they have attained everything possible in their spiritual lives. Every believer needs to press on with alert spiritual expectancy, constantly claiming fresh resources, responding to further challenges and grasping new opportunities. The worst thing is to think that in some sense or other we have "arrived." Luther greatly admired the example of Bernard of Clairvaux. He was specially fond of Bernard's saying, "When we begin not to want to become better, we cease to be good." Luther's understanding of the Christian life is dynamic; the believer is constantly on the move. Those who do not press on vigorously, gradually slip back. He insists that any Christian who "does not go forward in God's way goes backward."[8]

For Luther, the making of a good Christian is the work of a lifetime. God is like a gifted sculptor who, at the beginning of his work, can see in his mind what he intends to make out of the unshaped, even unpromising material before him. One of Luther's gifted interpreters put it like this: "As the great artist sees the finished statue in the rough marble, so God sees already in the sinner, whom he justifies, the righteous man that he will make of him."[9]

Such supremely delicate work continues through the whole of life, so the worst thing is to settle down contentedly to mediocre Christian living. The Lord is continually luring us on to something higher and better: it is the devil's device to make us sleepy and complacent. Christians who wish to grow in grace constantly reach out to fresh experiences of God's grace at present just beyond their fingertips. They exalt God in the words of the hymn writer: "Glory to thee for all the grace I have not tasted yet."

The pursuit cannot be made in our own energy, relying solely on our slender resources. Believers are totally dependent on the power of the word and the work of the Spirit. The word of God will teach, correct, encourage and inspire us; the Spirit of God will empower us in our conflict with the devil, giving us "wisdom and strength to withstand him bravely and gain the victory."

Both qualities, wisdom and strength, are vital if we are to conquer temptation. The wisdom will come through the written word the Spirit gave, for "men spoke from God as they were carried along by the Holy Spirit" (2 Pet 1:21). The word makes us wise so that we *know* what is right; the Spirit guarantees the moral dynamic to *do* what is right.

Seek His Help

In the seventh petition, "deliver us from evil," Luther reflects on the "danger, uncertainty, faithlessness and evil" of his time. The days are hard and the temptations hazardous; for many, life is "full of sorrow and misfortune." He does not exaggerate. The two martyrs we have already mentioned were not alone in paying the supreme price for their faithfulness to God's word. Executions began soon after 1520 with the publication of the papal bull (*Exsurge Domine*), which denounced Luther's teaching. It ordered him to recant within two months or be condemned. In the summer of 1523, two Augustinian monks, transformed by the Reformer's message, were burned at the stake in Brussels. The following year Luther was writing to his friend George Spalatin about the execution of a Viennese merchant, Caspar Tauber, "beheaded and burned on account of the word of God." Those who passed on Luther's books were specially vulnerable; in Budapest a Christian bookseller "was burned at the stake, together with his books which were placed around him, and he suffered most courageously for the Lord."

Given such life-threatening conditions, Luther prays that he and his fellow believers will not "lose heart nor fear death, but with steadfast faith" put their lives into the hands of God. It is a moving plea for courage in this life and confidence about the next.

Some Christians in our own time risk their lives for the cause of Christ. Those who witness for Christ in hazardous places deserve the prayerful support of their Christian partners in safer parts of the world. Some of our fellow Christians in China know what it is to live "under the cross," and there are other countries where our partners endure deprivation, imprisonment, exile or death for Jesus. Martyrs are not confined to a bygone age. Heroic people still suffer for him. They should be constantly upheld by the prayers of people they may never meet this side of heaven.

THE PARTNERSHIP OF PRAYER

When Luther completes his meditation on the seven petitions in the Lord's Prayer, he urges his friend to remember that when he prays, he is not kneeling in the presence of God as a solitary petitioner. Luther glories in the impossibility of loneliness at the place of prayer. God listens intently to him as though there were no one else speaking; but because he is omniscient, omnipresent and omnipotent, he welcomes thousands to his footstool. They can take heart that, although nobody else may be physically present while they pray, they are never alone when they come to God:

> Remember that you are not kneeling or standing there alone,
> but that all Christendom, all devout Christians are standing

there with you and you with them in one unanimous, united prayer which God cannot ignore.

How richly comforting that one sentence must have been to Peter Beskendorf as he clutched this little book in the isolation of exile. Compulsorily removed from home and family, ashamed and guilty over the sin of an unguarded moment, there was little left but the choice thought that, as he prayed, believers he would never see were crowding around, unitedly assuring him of forgiveness, peace and hope.

THE EFFECTIVENESS OF PRAYER

Another great certainty Luther shares about prayer is that not only is the petitioner surrounded by an invisible multitude, but he is also assured that his prayer has been heard. He is exhorted to say a confident "amen" to the prayer that has been offered,

> never doubting that God is surely listening to you with all grace and saying Yes to your prayer. . . . And never leave off praying without having said or thought: There now, this prayer has been heard by God; this I know of a certainty. This is what "Amen" means.

Praying men and women need not feel lonely as they pray; they are surrounded by an invisible but indisputable throng of believing companions. Nor is there cause for despondency that the exercise might be useless; every prayer is attentively heard by a loving Father who hears the cry of his needy children. His yearning that they talk with him far exceeds their best desire for prayer.

THE ATTENTIVENESS OF PRAYER

Luther emphasises that there is more to prayer than talk. When Christians enter the audience chamber of God, they listen carefully to what he says. Luther believes that while we pray, the Holy Spirit exercises his most persuasive ministry as our Teacher. It is vital that we do not crowd our prayer times with excessive words or laboriously work our way through well-organised patterns, even one based on the Lord's Prayer. We can be so busy, hurrying on to the next stage in our prearranged scheme that we forget that God may want to share something with us. So, Luther says, if "rich, good thoughts come" while we are praying with the aid of one petition, then

> one should let the other prayers go and give place to these thoughts. Listen to them in silence and on no account suppress them, for here the Holy Spirit himself is preaching to us, and a single word of his preaching is worth more than a thousand of our own prayers. I have often learned more in one prayer than I could have obtained from much reading and pondering.

Lecturing to his students on the message of the prophet Zechariah, he said that if we want God to hear our prayers, "we must first listen to the word of the Lord. Otherwise he will not listen, even though you weep and cry out—even if you burst."[10]

THE REVERENCE OF PRAYER

Luther had a delightful sense of humour and makes excellent use of it when he warns about the appalling practice of gabbling prayers without giving serious thought to what is being said. Few can escape the criticism. To drive his point home, he uses two illustrations, introducing us to the busy priest and the careless hairdresser.

The busy priest has a certain amount of religious material he must work his way through as he says his prayers at home, but his mind is elsewhere, continually absorbed with other things. He prattles away with familiar jargon, and preset phrases fall easily from his lips, but he is really thinking about the domestic chores, fretful lest his servants are wasting their time while his back is turned. Luther does not paint the picture as a mocking critic, but as one who knows the danger:

> What else is it but to tempt God if the mouth babbles and the heart be wandering elsewhere? It is like the priest who prayed in this way:

> > *Make haste, O God, to deliver me.*
> > Servant, have you unhitched the horses?
> > *Make haste to help me, O Lord.*
> > Maid, go milk the cow.
> > *Glory be to the Father and to*
> > *the Son and to the Holy Ghost.*
> > Run, boy, pox upon you!

Luther adds:

> I heard this kind of prayer often when I was under the papacy; and almost all their prayers are like that. This is only to mock God, and it would be better just to play at it, if they cannot or will not do any better than this.

Luther is haunted by experiences of that kind. He recalled with painful intensity his first visit to Rome as a young priest, overwhelmed with a sense of rich privilege, intent on bringing his heartfelt devotion to the celebration of the mass. But inside St Peter's, his Italian colleagues were impatient; he was not getting on with it quickly enough. "*Passa, passa,*" they called to him: "Get a move on."

Yet Luther is too honest a man simply to blame others; he knows that there have been times in his own life when he has been equally irreverent:

> Unfortunately, in my day, I myself prayed these canonical hours many a time in such a way that the psalm or the hour

was over before I was conscious whether I was at the beginning or the middle.

Luther knows, of course, that not all priests act like the one he has mentioned, "who jumbled his chores and his prayers together"; but, like the rest of us, even if the distractions are not verbalised, they "do this in the thoughts of their hearts."

> They go rambling on and when they are done, they do not know what they have said or covered. They start off with *Laudate* and in less than no time they are off in lubberland.

What an embarrassment if our wandering thoughts were projected onto a massive screen for others to view! One can hardly imagine "a more comical spectacle than one would see if it were possible to see the thoughts which a cold, irreverent heart will botch together." How important, Luther says, that we weigh our words when we pray, ponder our sentences, realise that we are in the presence of a God who reads hearts and knows what we really believe and feel.

His second illustration has Peter Beskendorf and his occupation uppermost in mind; it presses home the same point about the need for undivided attention:

> So, a good, clever barber must have his thoughts, mind, and eyes concentrated upon the razor and the beard and not forget where he is in his stroke and shave. If he keeps talking or looking around or thinking of something else, he is likely to cut a man's mouth or nose, or even his throat.

Beskendorf must have chuckled at the picture of the careless cut-throat barber, but Luther underlines his point by insisting that "anything that is to be done well ought to occupy the whole man with all his faculties and members." He quotes a familiar saying: "He who thinks of many things thinks of nothing and accomplishes no good." So, "how much more must prayer possess the heart exclusively and completely if it is to be good prayer."

Luther brings this section to a close by extolling the virtues and exposing the dangers of the Lord's Prayer. He says that he "can never get enough of it." He drinks it like a little child and devours it eagerly like an old man enjoying a good meal. "To me it is the best of all prayers, even above the Psalms, though I love them very much."

Though he uses the Lord's Prayer to provide a structure for his own prayers, he has one regret about it. His difficulty is not about its words, for "the true Master taught and composed it," but about its users. Scurrying through its majestic sentences, they mangle it to death: "It is a thousand pities that such a prayer of such a Master should be babbled and gabbled without any reverence throughout all the world."

It is tragic that many people "repeat the Lord's Prayer perhaps several thousand times a year, and if they prayed it this way for a thousand years they would still not have tasted nor prayed a single jot or tittle of it." Luther says that the Lord's Prayer is "the greatest martyr on earth, for everybody tortures and abuses it while few cherish and use it joyfully as it should be used." He says that the same can be said for God's name, repetitively interjected in the prayers of unthinking people; and much the same can be said about God's word, carelessly bandied about without serious thought concerning the immense value of every telling phrase.

THE RESOURCES OF PRAYER

Luther continues to share his own practice of prayer by explaining that, if he has "time and opportunity after the Lord's Prayer," he does the same with the Ten Commandments, producing from each "a garland of four twisted strands":

> I take each commandment first as teaching, which is what it actually is, and reflect on what our Lord God so earnestly requires of me here. Secondly, I make of it a thanksgiving. Thirdly, a confession. Fourthly, a prayer.

He looks on these four parts to each of his prayers as four books, "as a little book of teaching, a hymn book, a book of confession, and a prayer book." As he meditates on each commandment, he discerns how these verses might inform his mind, inspire his praise, expose his sins and direct his prayers.

Once again he insists that we should not use this fourfold plan mechanically, doggedly trudging through it with every single commandment: "See to it that you do not undertake all of it or too much of it, lest your spirit become weary." The value of a prayer has little to do with its length. It is judged by its dependence and sincerity: "A good prayer need not be long or drawn out, but rather should be frequent and ardent."

Luther says he uses his four-books structure to "strike a spark" in his heart. It is sufficient just to stay within one commandment, or "seize upon one part or even half of one part" if, while meditating and praying, the heart becomes warmed, the mind stimulated and the will directed to action. Once more he gives prominence to the Spirit's work in meditation. He is our incisive Teacher: he will "strike a spark . . . and will go on teaching in your heart if it is conformed to God's word and cleared of foreign concerns and thoughts."

As with the Lord's Prayer, Luther gives a series of examples of how he draws material for his four books from the commandments, itemising the truths that emerge in his meditations. Without repeating all his findings, I offer some examples of how he develops the theme.

Searching for material for his four books of teaching, thanksgiving, confession and prayer, he begins by looking at the first commandment: "I am the Lord your God. . . . You shall have no other gods before me."

This verse's lesson book has declared the greatness and uniqueness of God; it has taught the Reformer that he "must have sincere confidence in him in all things," and that it is God's "earnest purpose" to be Luther's God. Such a relationship demands his total allegiance: "My heart must neither build upon nor trust in anything else, be it goods, honour, wisdom, power or any created thing."

The praise theme here for inclusion in Luther's personal hymn book is that of thanksgiving to such a generous and reliable God. He is grateful for

> his unfathomable mercy, that has in so fatherly a way come down to me, a lost creature, and that, unasked and unbidden, without any merit on my part, he offers to be my God, to accept me, and be my comfort, refuge, help, and strength in every time of need. . . . Who can ever thank him enough for this?

With this commandment before him, Luther's confession book records his "great sinfulness and unthankfulness in . . . so enormously provoking his wrath with countless idolatries." For these sins, Luther repents and prays for forgiveness.

Inspired by this opening commandment, the Reformer's prayer book asks God for a better understanding of this teaching "day by day and with sincere trust to walk in accord with it." He prays:

> Watch over my heart that I may no longer be so thoughtless and unthankful, that I may seek none other gods nor comfort on earth or in any creature, but rather cleave only to thee, my only God, dear Lord, God and Father. Amen.

When he turns to the commandment about not taking God's name in vain, the lesson book insists that he is not to be proud or seek his own honour or name. This teaching rebukes our arrogance and self-assertiveness; true believers make it their "whole honour and pride" that such a God is their God.

Here, the hymn book encourages us to rejoice that we can be called by his name, as God's servant, creature, child, ambassador, so encouraging our sense of rich privilege. This commandment also inspires gratitude that, in all the experiences of life, God's unique name is a strong tower, "a mighty fortress . . . to which the righteous man flees and is safe" (Prov 18:10).

At this point his confession book acknowledges that he has

"not only failed to call upon, praise and honour his holy name" but that he has also been ungrateful for God's gifts of thought and speech and "misused his name for all kinds of shame and sin by swearing, lying, deceiving."

His prayer book includes a petition that he may "learn this commandment well and guard against this shameful unthankfulness . . . that I may be found grateful and in true fear and honouring of his name."

In similar fashion Luther goes through each of the commandments. As he reverently meditates on these familiar words, he draws more and more material from each of them for his four books. Time and again, the Spirit "strikes a spark" in his heart that causes him to linger and listen so that, being taught, he can adore God, receive his pardon and seek his power.

In later editions of the book he offers some helpful examples to show how the Creed might be similarly used, making of it another "four-stranded garland."

THE AFFIRMATIONS OF PRAYER

Prayer is not simply learning, thanking, confessing and asking; it is also gratefully affirming in the presence of God all we believe about him. Credal affirmations and catechisms were of immense importance in the sixteenth-century Reformation. Luther knew it would be unconstructive merely to criticise Catholic doctrine. Protestant believers must declare what they truly believed. So, in later editions of his book, Luther closes by meditating on the three great articles of the Creed with their majestic themes of God the Creator, Christ the Redeemer and the Holy Spirit the Sanctifier.

Affirming Our Confidence in God

As he reflects on the words, "I believe in God the Father Almighty, Maker of heaven and earth," one theme after another cries out for further contemplative meditation, such as the character of God, the nature of our humanity ("what you are, where you come from") and the wonder of creation, "the handiwork of God." To reflect on this teaching is to be reminded of our total indebtedness to the God who has made us (Creator) and loves us (Father). It reminds us that of ourselves we "are nothing . . . can do nothing" and "are capable of nothing." In making us, God generously gave us the breath we breathe, and it can be lost within seconds: "At any moment he can return you to nothingness."

As a theme for praise in the hymn book, this article of the Creed encourages us to give thanks "that by God's goodness we have been created out of nothing and daily preserved from nothingness—a fair creature of body and soul, reason, five senses," and that humanity is special in creation.

This truth prompts an item in our confession book, deploring our "unbelief and unthankfulness in not having taken this to heart, nor believed, regarded, or acknowledged it," making us "much worse than the dumb animals." The two greatest sins are ingratitude and idolatry: failing to recognise God as God and, in the inevitable vacuum, setting up ourselves in God's place. In Gordon Rupp's words, the Reformer "insists that human ingratitude is the beginning of the human disaster." Luther warns us to "take note of the order of the stages of perdition. The first is ingratitude. . . . The second is vanity: one feeds on one's own self."[11]

How swiftly ungrateful humanity becomes idolatrous, and self-worship is the worst and most prevalent form of idolatry. We become obsessed with the exaltation of our own ideas, the assertion of our own will and the satisfaction of our own desires. In his exposition of Romans, Luther put it like this:

> Scripture describes man as curved in upon himself to such an extent that he bends not only physical but also spiritual goods toward himself, seeking himself in all things . . . man loves himself above everything else, even above God. . . . [Man] is finally and ultimately concerned only for himself . . . [and the flesh] enjoys only itself and uses everyone else, even God.[12]

With this credal article in mind, believers look away from themselves, including in their prayer book the petition that, released from self-idolatry, they may have a "true, confident faith," rejoicing in such a bountiful Creator and trusting such a generous Father.

Affirming Our Security in Christ

When Luther comes to the second article, with its confession of Christ and his unique work of redemption, he specially focuses on the believer's assurance. Here is firm Protestant doctrine standing in stark contrast to Catholic uncertainty and hesitancy about the Christian's salvation. If we recognise that God is our Creator, then we may know with the same degree of certainty that Christ is our Saviour and Redeemer:

> Just as you had in the first article to count yourself a creature of God and never doubt it, so here, too, you must count yourself among the redeemed and never doubt it. Of all the words in it you must put first the word "our"; Jesus Christ, *our* Lord, suffered for *us*, died for *us*, rose again for *us*, so that everything is for us and applies to us, and you, too, are included in that "our." So the word is given to us personally.

The great truth of Christian assurance in the lesson book will ensure that the hymn book carries a psalm of gratitude, so that as confident believers we may "give hearty thanks for this grace and be joyful over such redemption."

The confession book will record with genuine sorrow those times when we may have seriously doubted this message of grace and certainty, foolishly relying on "countless works" of our own to earn our salvation.

The prayer book item will seek God's help that we may be preserved "in true, pure faith in Christ" right through to the end of our life on earth.

Affirming Our Dependence on the Spirit

When Luther meditates on the third article about the work of the Holy Spirit in sanctification, he focuses on the life of God's redeemed people in the church. He rightly emphasises the corporate aspects of evangelical faith that can become narrowly individualistic. Salvation must be understood in personal terms, of course. Nobody was more insistent on that than Luther. His comment on Paul's words in Galatians 2:20, "the Son of God who loved me, and gave himself for me," is classic:

> Read therefore with great vehemency these words "ME" and "FOR ME," and so inwardly practise with yourself that you with a sure faith may conceive and print this "ME" in your heart, and apply it to yourself, not doubting but that you are of the number to whom this word "ME" belongs; also that Christ had not only loved Peter and Paul and given himself for them, but that the same grace which is comprehended in this "ME" as well pertains and comes to us, as to them.[13]

Yet, for all his clear assurance of personal salvation, Luther does not make the mistake of suggesting that it is thereby individual salvation. Belonging to Christ, we are part of his body, the church. So Luther's manual of prayer closes with a reminder that "where the holy Christian church is, there you find God the Creator, God the Redeemer, and God the Holy Ghost, who daily sanctifies through the forgiveness of sins."

Inevitably, Luther wants to define the church as the place "where God's word concerning this faith is rightly preached and confessed." "Here again," he tells his barber, "you have much to meditate upon of all that the Holy Spirit performs every day in the church, and so on."

The hymn book entry must include praise that we too "have been called and have come into this church," while the confession book laments those times of "unbelief and unthankfulness in not having regarded all this."

Luther knows that, in the face of increasing opposition and persecution his readers must plead for qualities of unswerving loyalty and tenacity. His closing words form a prayer book entry in which he urges his reader to

> ... pray for the right, steadfast faith that endures and abides until you come to that place where everything will remain eternally, that is, after the resurrection of the dead in everlasting life. Amen.

When Peter Beskendorf first received this little book from his customer, Martin Luther, life was going well for him. He had a comfortable home, secure family, reasonably successful business, a host of good friends and a nearby church where his faith was regularly nourished and sustained by Luther's fine expository ministry. Within a short space of time, all that was gone. In the bleakness of exile, all he could do was cast himself utterly upon God and upon the faith that Luther's book had sought to inform, stimulate and encourage.

Luther's *A Simple Way to Pray* had taught him to read his Bible, not mechanically and hurriedly, but quietly and meditatively, finding within Scripture rich material for prayer to fill the pages of his four books. Like every other Christian, Peter Beskendorf needed an alert mind to receive God's teaching, a thankful heart to appreciate his blessings, a penitent spirit to admit his faults and the wisdom to seek fresh grace for each succeeding day. Commenting on the Reformer's spirituality, the Catholic historian Joseph Lortz says:

> Luther possessed a mighty power of prayer. He was rooted in God; he knew the thoughts which God has made accessible to us through revelation in such depth, bore them about with him as such living possessions, that he never had to jump over any ditch before beginning to speak with God or about God.[14]

Luther believed that to be a Christian is to pray. For him, the very idea of a prayerless Christian was a contradiction in terms:

"As a shoemaker makes a shoe, and a tailor makes a coat, so a Christian ought to pray. Prayer is the daily business of a Christian."[15]

When Luther shared the pattern of his own prayer life with the Wittenberg hairdresser, he gave to Christians throughout the centuries choice teaching about the believer's greatest privilege—immediate access into the presence of a God who always welcomes us with joy.

.†.

JOHN BUNYAN

Grace Abounding
to the Chief of Sinners

I Am
for Going On

Luther maintained that three things make a good minister—prayer, meditation and suffering. Actually, all three feature in the spiritual development of any mature Christian, whether a minister or not. We have seen that prayer was uppermost in Luther's message to Peter Beskendorf, and Augustine's *Confessions* is one adoring prayer from beginning to end. So as we turn to Bunyan, we focus on Luther's second theme—meditation. In this chapter we shall look at the book in which Bunyan meditated on the love and transforming power of Christ, *Grace Abounding to the Chief of Sinners*, and, as we do so, consider ways in which we might use some of the book's main themes to encourage our own meditation on God's goodness to us. But first a brief introduction to the writer of this influential spiritual classic.

Born at Elstow, Bedfordshire, in 1628, John Bunyan came from a relatively poor family. When barely in his midteens, he was one of Cromwell's soldiers in the Civil War. Once hostilities were over, he worked as a tinker or brazier, developing skills he had learned from his father and travelling to many of the small towns and villages of the county. Setting out on journeys was the pattern of daily life for Bunyan, and when imprisonment prevented him from travelling, he spent a good deal of his time reflecting on the message of Scripture, pursuing an imaginative journey as he meditated on the challenge, temptations and benefits of the Christian life. That journey motif provided the literary structure for an extended allegory that became one of the most famous books in the world, *Pilgrim's Progress*. The pilgrim's adventures, hazards and achievements were the fruit of Bunyan's frequent meditation on the teaching of the Bible as well as on personal and corporate Christian experience.

Brought to faith in his midtwenties, Bunyan became a member of the Independent Church in Bedford under the pastoral leadership of John Gifford. His own gifts as a preacher were soon recognised and encouraged by his fellow members, but laws had been passed that prevented nonconformist believers from meeting regularly for worship, teaching and witness.

In 1660 he was imprisoned for preaching and thereby lost his freedom for the next twelve years. During that long period, he gave himself to the ministry of writing, was able to do some preaching in jail, and, with the help of an obliging jailer, had occasional opportunities to leave the prison for a few hours to encourage his persecuted fellow believers as they met secretly in barns, fields and woods in various parts of the county.

Only a couple of months before his release from jail in 1672, the Bedford church invited their now well-known member to become their next pastor. Although his *Grace Abounding* was written prior to his appointment to pastoral leadership, it is clear that its author had a warm pastoral heart. Both in prison and outside it, he often had the opportunity to care for people spiritually, and in his book he wants to help men and women in their spiritual need. His personal experience of God's grace invites the reader to think specifically about how grace is recalled, received and shared.

RECALLING GOD'S GRACE

When Bunyan set aside time in prison to write his testimony, he was following a precedent firmly established in English Puritanism. The writing of spiritual autobiography and the keeping of journals and diaries increased by leaps and bounds during the seventeenth century and was fairly common when Bunyan recorded the traumatic details of his own spiritual journey. Though separated by centuries, Augustine and Bunyan were united in the belief that there is great spiritual value in preparing a detailed account of God's goodness to them personally. We might benefit from their example.

Those twelve years in jail provided Bunyan with ample opportunity for quiet recollection and reflection. Even in that uncongenial environment, his "mind was free to study Christ":

> For though men keep my outward man
> Within their locks and bars
> Yet by the faith of Christ I can
> Mount higher than the stars.[1]

In the early years of his imprisonment, he had time to compose simple verses that expressed his new experience; the titles of these published poems, *Profitable Meditations* (1661) and *Prison Meditations* (1663), indicate the importance for Bunyan of this neglected aspect of Christian prayer and devotion. In *Grace Abounding* he tells us that when he first began to give serious thought to the Christian message, he had a great desire for "a continual meditating" on the Scriptures and "on all other good things" that he had heard or read about[2] and that in those days he was "never out of the Bible, either by reading or meditation," that he might discover the "way to Heaven and Glory."[3] The practice of meditation deserves a more prominent place in contemporary teaching about the spiritual life. Our spiritual forefathers derived immense benefit from it. Calvin often mentioned the importance of meditation in his sermons and biblical commentaries as well as in his famous *Institutes of the Christian Religion*,[4] and through the Puritans Bunyan was influenced by Calvin as well as Luther. Encouraged by their example, we ought now to look at the meaning and purpose of meditation.

The Meaning of Meditation

Meditation is an opportunity for personal communion with God by which we endeavour to concentrate on him, giving undistracted thought to his nature, acts, word and will for our lives. It is a non-vocal form of prayer, an experience of stillness and contemplation, when we focus our minds on our triune God as he is revealed in Scripture, history and personal experience. By this means we seek to extend our knowledge of him, increase our love for him and commitment to him. If we love somebody very much, our love and the pleasure we derive from our relationship are not remotely confined to those times when we are talking to the person. We think about loved ones when we are away from them, about what they mean to us, how deeply indebted we are to them, and whether there is anything we might do to further express our continuing closeness. Meditation is rather like that. It is our opportunity to think deeply about God's love for us and our love for him—its reality, privilege, implications and consequences.

The Puritans insisted on firm biblical authority for their patterns of devotion and prayer. When writing about meditation, they frequently quoted two verses of Old Testament Scripture. One, the Bible's first reference to meditation (Gen 24:63), describes an occasion when Isaac "went out *to the field* one evening to meditate." The Puritans believed it could be uplifting and inspiring to meditate outdoors. Some of Bunyan's transforming thoughts came to him while he walked through the Bedfordshire countryside.

We might learn from him and the Puritans in that respect, perhaps discovering some quiet, restful place outdoors where we too can reflect on the majesty, wisdom, generosity and loving providence of God. Some people have found that they can do that best while on a leisurely country walk, contemplating the wonder of creation and, at the same time, rejuvenating their bodies, filling their lungs with good fresh air. Richard Sibbes believed that "every creature has a beam of God's glory in it." He held that "everything is from the Holy Spirit" who "elevates nature above itself, and sets a spiritual stamp, and puts divine qualities upon it." Perhaps we could create opportunities to discern those qualities and fresh aspects of that glory by meditating in a secluded garden or while looking out on some magnificent rural landscape, discovering afresh with Sibbes that "the whole world is a theatre of the glory of God."[5] Francis Thompson's "No Strange Land" conveys a necessary rebuke:

> 'Tis ye, 'tis your estrangéd faces,
> That miss the many-splendoured thing.

We all need "space" for contemplation so that in an unhurried context we can turn our minds to the highest and best things, and emerge as people better equipped to serve God in his world. The gospels frequently tell us about times when Christ created opportunities for personal prayer outdoors, sometimes doing it at the cost of sleep (Mk 1:35). He often withdrew to a quiet place where he could appreciate the solitude and feed his soul by essential communion with his Father. Life was exceptionally busy for him, with inevitable claims upon his time and constant interruptions, but he "often withdrew to lonely places and prayed" (Lk 5:16). What was vital for him can hardly be optional for us.

For their second authority for meditation, the Puritans turned to the familiar description of a godly believer in the first psalm as one who delights in God's word and meditates on its teaching day and night (Ps 1:2). Those two biblical references to meditation helped them to focus on God's revelation in the created world and in the written word, both portrayed side by side in that divine meditation that we know as Psalm 19 where "the heavens declare the glory of God" and the trustworthy "statutes of the Lord" are found to be "more precious than gold."

With other seventeenth-century Christians, Bunyan believed that for this spiritual exercise to be profitable, discipline was needed to allocate time to think deeply about what God is saying to us and then set down in writing the result of our meditation. It is not a form of religious escapism; believers who practise it regularly emerge from their time spent with God as better people, more prepared and equipped to serve him in the world. Bunyan and his contemporaries held that meditation had a threefold purpose: It created specific opportunities to exalt God, encourage ourselves and help others.

The Purpose of Meditation

That first "praise" element is important for us too, for although we may all be aware of our indebtedness to God, it is possible to ignore or overlook particular ways in which the Lord has been good to us and, in the rush of hurried hectic days, fail to notice, let alone record, how generous God has been to us. During 1879, the hymn-writer Frances Ridley Havergal kept a "Journal of Mercies." Every evening she wrote down one thing for which in that day she was specially grateful to God. Her deliberate decision to limit it to a single entry meant that, in the process of selection, one thing after another jostled for a place in her mind as she reflected on what God had done for her in that particular day. This awareness of the multiplicity of grace naturally encouraged her gratitude and inspired her adoration at the end of the day.[6]

When Augustine wrote his *Confessions* in the form of that extended meditative prayer, he also said that his primary aim was to glorify God. He asked that the Lord would help him to remember the "past twistings" of his "mistaken life" so that, recalling his experience, he might offer everything as a "sacrifice" to the God who had pursued and transformed him. Augustine hoped that by his story he might be "stirring up love" for God, not only in himself but in those who read his book so that all his readers might say, "Great is the Lord and highly worthy to be praised."[7] Bunyan had an identical aim. He shared his very different experience in *Grace Abounding* "that thereby the goodness and bounty of God towards me, may be the more advanced and magnified." His predominant desire was to "magnify the Heavenly Majesty."

Bunyan also believed that meditation is one way of encouraging ourselves. While reading the Samson narrative, it occurred to him that by recalling God's mercy in former days, he too was sharing "a drop of that honey" that he had "taken out of the carcass of a lion" (Judg 14:5-8). Writing helped him to remember the abundant mercy of God across the years: "I have eaten thereof myself, and am much refreshed thereby." Bunyan's confinement in Bedford gaol was in some sense like Samson's life-threatening encounter with the lion; unexpectedly good things had come out of it. Imprisonment, though cruel, unjust, frustrating and uncomfortable, was not totally bad; like other adverse experiences, it could be used to exalt God, enrich his own life and inspire others. Adversities can become eloquent messengers of an all-sufficient God.

Bunyan maintained that there was good biblical precedent for relating and recording our experience of God's goodness. It was at God's command that Moses wrote about the various stages of Israel's wilderness journey (Num 33:2). Bunyan hoped that as people reflect on his pilgrimage of faith they too "may be put in remembrance of what he has done for their souls, by reading his work upon me." He related other occasions in Scripture when past blessings encouraged present hope. For example, when David asked if he might fight the Philistine giant, he told King Saul about the help God gave him in times of serious danger, as on those threatening occasions when the young shepherd confronted both lion and bear. Recollection of earlier deliverances inspires new confidence.

Can Bunyan's readers not do the same? Surely they too have experiences of the mercy of God that they can recall, share with others and possibly set down in writing: "My dear children, call to mind the former days . . . remember also your songs in the night . . . for there is treasure hid."

Bunyan remembered certain places and localities where God had made himself known to him when he was a pained and bewildered seeker. His narrative is punctuated with the mention of homes, highways, fields and hedges in Bedfordshire where God's truth broke into his troubled mind with unforgettable appeal. Cannot the believing friends who read his book recall similar encounters with the God of all grace? "Have you forgot the Close, the Milk-house, the Stable, the Barn and the like, where God did visit your soul?"

But the recording of experience is not simply to encourage ourselves. Bunyan also wrote to help others. He reminded his readers that in the New Testament, Paul often thought "of that day and that hour, in the which he did first meet with grace."[8] His testimony to God's mercy in the life of a blaspheming persecutor is recorded in different contexts as a means of magnifying the patient love of God and helping others to realise that nobody is too bad to receive new life in Jesus (Acts 9:1-19; 22:1-22; 26:1-23; 1 Tim 1:12-16).

Bunyan naturally hoped that, like the apostle's testimony, his book would make an evangelistic impact, bringing people to faith in Christ, but its primary message was for Christians who were experiencing hard times. It is not the story of an immediate dramatic conversion in which the disturbed soul is suddenly released from the burden of sin, passing in a moment of revelation from disturbing darkness to blazing light. It is an account of the long, agonising struggle of a man with a "wounded conscience," vividly told in the hope that the story of his conflict may help others. They too may be experiencing fierce temptation, perhaps failures similar to his own, and, though rarely able to preach to them now that he was in prison, he could help them through his writing by sharing his account of God's goodness to a man in need. If they have "sinned against the light," or are "tempted to blaspheme," if they feel despondent or think that God is fighting against them and that heaven is hid from their eyes, they may derive comfort from the realisation that somebody whose heroism they admire has been through those troubles also, and that "out of them all the Lord delivered" him. He hoped that "others may be put in remembrance" of what God has done for their souls by reading his personal account of the persistent love of God.

As Bunyan relates his story, a number of key themes emerge in the narrative. They are not hurriedly set down in writing. He had been a prisoner for about six years when the book was published. His work is the fruit of months of quiet recollection of the infinite tenderness of a loving God. Perhaps his meditation on these great biblical truths might also become the basis for a written account of "grace abounding" in our own lives. Possibly we might find a quiet period and place where we can think in an unhurried way about what God has done for us and then write down the story of God's dealings with us personally.

Many of the themes in Bunyan's narrative will doubtless form part of our own story, but we need not confine ourselves to those attributes of God's nature and facets of Christian experience that appealed to him. No individual person has a monopoly of the grace of God. Our story is not going to be exactly like his, but it will doubtless reflect different, possibly complementary, themes. But giving time to meditate on past and present experience, what Scripture has said and continues to say to us, and what we have learned and continue to receive from other Christians, will surely cause us to exalt God and encourage ourselves. Moreover, as we meditate, it may also prompt us to consider practical ways in which we can help others either in their quest for personal faith or in their spiritual pilgrimage in difficult times (Ps 66:16-20).

Our human personalities are extraordinarily different, and God does not deal with us in a rigidly stereotyped fashion. There is only one gospel, but the Lord has a variety of different means by which he wins the allegiance of self-centred and rebellious minds. In pastoral experience over many years, Baxter discovered that "God breaketh not all men's hearts alike."[9] The account of God's dealings with John Bunyan should encourage us to marvel at the different ways in which he has conveyed his grace to us and inspire our gratitude for the patience and persistence of his love and mercy.

RECEIVING GOD'S GRACE

As Bunyan meditated on God's grace in his own life, he came to see that it had come to him by means of a wounded conscience, through the reading of his Bible, the encouragement of friends, the contribution of Christian books, and through inspired preaching.

A Wounded Conscience

Bunyan's personal experience of God's grace was transmitted inwardly by a painfully extended experience, through what he describes as a "wounded conscience." As a young man, he had been a disruptive influence in the local community, and at that time religious things were unattractive to him: "But God did not utterly leave me, but followed me still."[10] After a period during which his interests were diverted to nominal religious practices and zealous church attendance, his heart and mind became profoundly disturbed as he reflected seriously on his earlier moral failure and spiritual indifference. Things began to change.

One of the prominent aspects of Puritan teaching about meditation was that it could be used as part of a process of necessary exposure, showing individual seekers how much they stood in need of the grace of God. God's word becomes like a mirror, or roving searchlight, revealing what we are really like in God's sight, probing the hidden depths of our submerged antagonism to the things of God. In Bunyan's case the process was painful and prolonged. He began to fear that he was not forgiven, especially after a momentary experience in which he appeared to turn Christ away from his life. The torment of his possible rejection went on month after month, hardly relieved except by occasional verses of Scripture that brought only momentary comfort.

At first he was disappointed about the mistakes he had made in earlier life, but as the months went by, his impressionable mind became concerned about issues more serious than swearing and Sabbath-breaking. He feared that he had grieved God so much that there might be no hope of pardon and peace. His tortured spirit ranged far and wide among the huge questions that have troubled devout men and women across the centuries: What if he was not included among the elect? How can anybody possibly tell whether they belong to God or not?[11] Suppose the day of grace has already passed? "How if you have overstood [or missed] the time of mercy?"[12] What if God does not exist and all religion is nothing but the fruit of a fertile imagination and the Bible nothing but a collection of valueless fables?[13] And questions that seem more dominant in a secularised society like ours: What if other major world religions are just as valid as Christianity? And "How if all our Faith, and Christ, and Scriptures, should be but a think-so too?"[14]

Some of his Christian friends tried to help him as he wrestled with such questions and quoted verses from Paul, which only gave rise to fresh uncertainties: What if the apostle was himself deluded, even damaging, and, as a "subtle and cunning man," had travelled the first-century world simply "to undo and destroy his fellows"?[15]

Oppressive thoughts of this nature did not pay fleeting visits to his enquiring mind but took him over like hostile inward foes, urging him to blaspheme. At such times he felt utterly powerless, as one swept away by an overwhelming whirlwind. Tormented by such notions, his alert imagination often produced some vivid picture, frequently drawn from rural life. At one time he said he felt like a helpless child in the grip of some gypsy, carried forcefully away from love and home. Village people always felt threatened when unknown strangers disturbed the predictable routine of a local community: "Kick sometimes I did, also scream and cry, but yet I was as bound in the wings of the temptation, and the wind would carry me away." If only he were a dog or toad, with no feeling for such things, "for they had no soul to perish under the everlasting weights of hell for sin, as mine was like to do."[16]

For about a year he was constantly beset with the temptation to reject Christ: "Sell him, sell him, sell him," and at times the devil convinced him that he had done such a thing. "Then I should be as tortured on a rack for whole days together." It is hardly surprising that, under such relentless pressure and fierce mental anguish, his sensitive spirit finally yielded, and the words rushed to the front of his mind to send Christ away from his life once and for all.

Immediately he was plunged into total gloom. Again turning

to familiar rural imagery, he felt like a bird shot from the top of a tree, plunging to the earth, lifeless and finished. He was a convicted criminal, bound over for eternal punishment. Profoundly disturbed, he found that a text from Hebrews pursued him like a menacing foe. It concerned Esau's plea in Old Testament times. When Esau wanted to inherit the blessing he had forfeited, he was not given a chance to repent, though he sought it with tears (Heb 12:17). The words haunted Bunyan.

He was the "profane person" of the Genesis narrative, and his lacerated soul agonised both at the thought of what he had done and its devastating consequences. He had deliberately refused the mercy of Christ by saying, "Let him go if he will"; like Esau, he would have no opportunity to repent "though he sought it carefully with tears."[17]

All this, its subsequent pain and discomfort, related in such vivid language, is harrowing even to read about, let alone experience. Peace eventually came, and the book that tormented eventually brought him cleansing and assurance. But, before moving to that, perhaps we ought to linger for a moment with this theme of meditation and its searching, probing, corrective influence in our Christian lives. We would not wish that anyone should go through Bunyan's months of unremitting conflict, spiritual desolation and sense of rejection, nevertheless, we can learn a great deal from his experience.

Such sad introspection and unrelieved guilt is certainly not the experience of every Christian believer, and there is no reason why it should be ours. There is little need for Bunyan's precise tortures to be reproduced artificially in our own lives. Our past may be different, but his experience is a searching challenge.

In the late twentieth century, we are probably in greater peril than Bunyan. Our danger is that of casualness and moral indifference. We are more likely to trivialise sin and dismiss or ignore its destructive potential in human life. We need a searching examination of our personal lives. Nearly every homemaker believes that the house deserves a spring clean. Cars have regular servicing.

Equipment at work and home is cleaned and checked so that its users are guarded against incipient danger. The gifted Methodist leader, W. E. Sangster, suggested that from time to time every believer needs "a spiritual checkup."[18]

To be effective, meditation ought to include that element of self-exposure, a willingness to probe into the concealed areas of our own lives and to ask searching questions to which we should not quickly respond. It is part of a divine scrutiny that can only become beneficial as we spend time in the presence of an all-seeing, holy and merciful God. It is not always easy for such probing to take place. Life is full for most of us, and there are plenty of protective mental barriers we subconsciously erect when an uncomfortable spiritual exercise approaches—frantic busyness, soothing procrastination, urgent preoccupation with important church work, criticism of others, more important assignments, necessary leisure, prolonged resentment about how things have turned out for us. Any of these become effective barriers that preclude serious reflection about our spiritual lives.

As we observe the way Bunyan submitted his life to honest scrutiny, it suggests possible lines of thought for a similar (though, we hope, more gentle) interrogation about our lives. As God's Spirit probed his life, he became aware of areas of failure that might easily have been overlooked. How could he possibly magnify God's mercy in saving him if he did not know how much he stood in need of that transformation? Our sins may not be his, but facing up to them is an essential aspect of confession and forgiveness. As he reflected on the past, Bunyan came to see that his life had been marred by a number of failures. I have selected six of them as examples of his willingness to examine his life in the light of God's word.

Indifference. In his earlier days, Bunyan was a damaging influence on other young people in the community. Until a local woman (far from moral herself) pointed it out to him, he had not been remotely troubled about it.[19] Have we hurt others by our conversation and conduct, not only by what we have done, but possibly by what we have failed to do? The effect our behaviour has upon others in our family, neighbourhood, at work or at church is not an issue about which any Christian can afford to be apathetic.

Ingratitude. In Bunyan's earlier life, God had been specially good to him, protecting him during several experiences when he might well have died, either by drowning, being bitten by a snake, or killed during a military exercise. But these providential mercies did nothing to awaken his soul spiritually. He did not thank God for protecting mercy but "grew more and more rebellious" and careless about his spiritual need. We too can take God's generosity and love for granted, and fail to notice how lovingly he has cared for us across the years.

Arrogance. He gained a superficial interest in spiritual things by regular attendance at his local church, even engaging in service as a bell-ringer. He enjoyed conversations about religious issues and claimed to be a "brisk talker"[20] about such matters. Pride was one of his problems. When his neighbours regarded him a devout man, it pleased him very much, but in his heart he knew himself to be "nothing but a poor painted hypocrite."[21] His facile talk was not matched by genuine experience. What we say may sometimes create the impression that we are further ahead spiritually than we are.

Irreverence. At times he deliberately put God to the test, insisting that miracles of his own choosing were to happen at the time he dictated, that puddles in the road might suddenly become dry, and empty holes immediately fill with water. He came to see that it was the devil's work to put such ridiculous ideas into his mind, and that his mistake was due to ignorance of God's word. Lack of submission to God's sovereign will often assumes these forms of pretentious dogmatism about how he ought to act in our lives.

Unbelief. Bunyan gradually realised that such presumptuous notions were nothing other than a refusal to accept the truth of God's word. Once when his wife was in childbirth, he prayed secretly for her relief. He told God that if the pain eased to give her rest that night, he would know that God truly reads the hearts of men and women. But it dawned on him later that it was wrong to lay down conditions of that kind. Scripture makes it clear that God *does* read the thoughts of our hearts (1 Cor 4:5; Heb 4:13), whether or not we have immediate answers to our specific prayers. He saw that it was similar to Gideon's improper demands about the fleece, "when he should have believed and ventured upon His Word."[22] At times we may be guilty of dictating to God how he must act in particular circumstances when it is more appropriate to declare our faith in his ability to do anything he wishes, surrender ourselves afresh to his sovereign purposes, and believe that he has more than one way of answering our prayers. His refusal to give precisely what we desire at the moment we demand it may be evidence of his love rather than indifference to our need.

Resentment. As he looked around the Bedford church, Bunyan began to feel that other people had all the blessings God was denying to him. He noticed that some "could rejoice, and bless God for Christ; and others, again, could quietly talk of, and with gladness remember, the word of God; while I only was in the storm or tempest."[23] If only he was somebody else. It is all too easy to fall into that trap of self-pity and ill-feeling, whereby we contrast our lives with those who appear to have a far better time in life. It is a foolish mistake. Nobody knows the secret pressures and tensions of other people, and, in any case, they may yet encounter difficulties that would test our faith to the limit. Our responsibility is to live at our best for God within the arena of life he has entrusted to us and to prove his goodness in it. We are not answerable for other people's actions, but we will be accountable for our own (Rom 14:10-12; 2 Cor 5:9-10).

Our reading of *Grace Abounding* could become spiritually transforming if, as well as understanding Bunyan's painful consciousness of sin, we became more sensitive to our own. Possibly we ought to make self-examination part of our experience of meditation. The results could well be:

- a deeper awareness of the purity and beauty of Christ by which alone our standards should be judged.
- a firmer hold on the unchanging promise of God's cleansing.

- a greater appreciation of the undeserved but assured miracle of forgiveness.
- a more alert perception of the Holy Spirit's ministry in exposing our sins and challenging our carelessness about moral and spiritual hazards.
- a more realistic estimate of our spiritual achievements.
- a more sensitive and sympathetic understanding of other people's failings.
- a more resolute determination to pray for those who are going through menacing times of spiritual uncertainty.

If meditation enables us to view ourselves more critically and creatively and think of others more compassionately, it will abundantly repay the time we allocate to it. If it provides a specific opportunity to make these lives of ours more open to God's power, Christ's love and the Spirit's holy presence, it will have accomplished a great deal in our spiritual lives and make our witness and service more effective in the world.

Bunyan discovered that the unique word that exposed his sin also explained its remedy. We now turn to another means by which God's grace invaded his troubled mind.

The Reading of His Bible

Grace Abounding is not only the testimony of a transformed sinner, but an exposition by a persuasive preacher. Bunyan did not want us to concentrate on him, but on the truth that changed him. He wrote in a time of fierce persecution. Nonconformist believers, able to meet only occasionally for their illegal gatherings, could at least open Scripture at their meal table in their own homes. Therefore, the Bible was central for Bunyan, and he wanted the reader of his book to emerge with a greater appreciation of the power, relevance and effectiveness of the biblical message.

However, we have seen already that Bunyan's anguish seemed heightened by the dual role played by Scripture in his quest for salvation; it both comforted and condemned. Several things strike us about the crucial role of the Bible in his emerging spirituality.

We are astonished, first of all, by his wide knowledge of both the Old and New Testaments. Here is a man who tells us that, only a few years earlier, he was not remotely interested in Christian things. Yet, within months it seems, he is accosted by Esau, haunted by Saul, harassed by Isaiah, taunted by Nebuchadnezzar, convicted by Peter, threatened by Judas and bewildered by Paul. Time was precious to this man; he had a family to support and worked hard for his living. Leaving home early in the morning, he travelled to the county's towns and scattered villages, visiting farms and cottages, repairing tools, simple farming equipment and household utensils. One cannot imagine there was much time for leisurely reading. How could a man like that acquire such a vast knowledge of Scripture and roam so widely through its pages, making perceptive comments about its many characters and their message?

We need to remember that his introduction to the Bible predates his meeting with the Bedford believers. Many people in that period were able to read even when they could not write. Hundreds of children had their first lessons in reading from the pages of a family Bible. Bunyan possessed such a Bible prior to meeting the Bedford pastor John Gifford and his friends, and it may have been in his family for decades. Children at this time could often read passages of Scripture with consummate ease. The wife of Oliver Heywood, a Presbyterian minister, could read "the hardest chapter in the Bible when she was but four years of age," and Oliver Sansom, a Berkshire Quaker, began to read when he was about six years old and did so well that in about four months "he could read a chapter in the Bible pretty readily."[24]

Once he began to attend services at the local parish church, Bunyan started reading the Bible for himself, especially the historical sections of the Old Testament, but as for Paul's letters he could not interest himself in them at all.[25] However, when he met up with his friends from the Bedford meeting things began to change. Their commitment to Scripture turned his mind to the Christian gospel.

He began to look at his Bible with new eyes. Paul's letters now became a special comfort[26] and he was increasingly captivated by the vitality and dynamism of God's unique word.

The Scripture was alive and active, "sharper than any double-edged sword" (Heb 4:12). He spent so much time with this book that his impressionable mind became permeated with its stories, teaching, promises and demands. The message came to him not merely visually as he carefully read its pages but almost audibly and with such compelling power that he could not possibly ignore what was said. He has favourite phrases to express the dynamic activity of God's word. Like a well-directed arrow, the truth could suddenly *dart* from heaven into his troubled soul.[27] As an eager messenger, it came *running* into his mind.[28] At times he was *followed* persistently by a saying from the gospels; it came hard on his heels, pleading with such persuasive power that he imagined someone was shouting to him from behind: "I turned my head over my shoulder ... that somebody had called after me that was half a mile behind me."[29]

Guilty and condemned, he found at times that a reassuring promise pursued him with tender appeal: "I have blotted out as a thick cloud thy transgressions." It made him stop in his tracks and look over his shoulder to see if he could discern that the God of grace was following him "with a pardon in his hand."[30]

For Bunyan the power of the word was urgent, compelling and inescapable, demanding a response. At times he longed to give it the complete trust and obedience it both warranted and demanded, but, for a man with a sensitive spirit, it seemed far more complicated than that. The conflict in his own soul seemed matched by a tension within Scripture itself. One verse invited him to believe; another denounced his unbelief. One biblical incident portrayed his eventual release; another foretold his inevitable doom. The repentant Peter said he could be "found"; hardened Esau warned he would be lost. The passages about apostasy in Hebrews were particularly harassing and seemed the only sentences to keep him out of heaven.[31]

In crisis, the discord became focused on two different Scripture verses, each locked in combat, battling for his soul. One lured him persuasively to heaven; the other cast him irrevocably into hell. Buffeted by these conflicts, he found the pain intolerable; he felt as though his heart would break under the strain of it. Paul's assurance of sufficient grace (2 Cor 12:9) was always countered by the remembrance of Esau's tears.[32]

Distressed and bewildered, he asked if there was any hope that "the Scriptures could agree in the salvation of my soul." The day came when it seemed that the two texts came forcefully upon him at the same time, and "at last that about Esau's birthright began to wax weak, and withdraw, and vanish; and this about the sufficiency of grace prevailed, with peace and joy."

His turbulent struggle became a parable to him that the Bible's necessarily serious words about "Law and Wrath must give place to the Word of Life and Grace." Here in measure was a reenactment of what happened on the Mount of Transfiguration: "Moses and Elijah must both vanish, and leave Christ and his saints alone."[33]

A promise of Christ brought the greatest peace. Esau's threat was silenced by the compelling invitation of Jesus: "And him that comes to me I will in no wise cast out." There were no exceptions. A single phrase was enough to awaken a rhapsody of exaltation: "O the comfort I had from this word, *in no wise*." He had not reached the end of the struggle, but this marked the beginning of peace. Assurance came to Bunyan by trusting Christ's unfailing promise and recalling his persistent love. Comforted by those mercifully inclusive words, "in no wise," he was given the courage to look his greatest fear in the face. Instead of running away like a terrified offender, he turned back to look honestly at what he had said about Jesus: "Let him go if he will." Why had those words tormented him so fiercely over many unhappy months? It was because he did not know enough about the one to whom they had been spoken.

He had not realised that, although the Saviour has the freedom to go, he had resolved not to do so. His love demands that he pursue rebellious sinners to their final hours. While life remains, hope continues. The New Testament letter that had troubled him most, with its severe warning about Esau, now conveyed its message of unlimited compassion: "Then the Scripture gave me hope: 'I will never leave you nor forsake you.' . . . 'O Lord,' I said, 'but I have left you'; then it answered again: But 'I will never leave you.'"[34] Accepting the promise of Hebrews 13:5 (and Josh 1:5), he found peace.

Applying God's word is a central theme in *Grace Abounding*. Bunyan shows that as he spent time with Scripture, it did three things for him. First, it exposed him as a man in great need. Then it pointed helpfully to needy biblical personalities whose lives had been transformed. Third, it revealed the God whose ability to meet their needs confirmed his eagerness to meet Bunyan's. His testimony to the crucial role of the Bible in the quest for faith is relevant to us as we look at similar ways of applying God's word to our daily lives.

First, as with Bunyan, there will be occasions when Scripture will make us feel decidedly ill at ease. It discloses the truth about us. If studied unhurriedly and meditatively, Scripture's realistic portraits of its characters begin to change, almost imperceptibly, into luminous mirrors. For the serious reader, the Bible does not simply describe the sins of others; it uncovers our own. Bunyan needed that near-scorching searchlight of the Esau passage to save him from the danger of rejecting God's gifts. Esau's willingness to forfeit his birthright for immediate satisfaction seemed to be a picture of Bunyan's agonised condition—a man who had said no to God's best gift. In Bunyan's case it seemed to reveal the worst of all sins, the possibility that he had spurned Christ's offer of forgiveness and new life. Yet, crucial as that exposure was, there was something more vital and urgent.

Next the seeker also needed the Bible's vivid description of help generously given to others. One of the glorious things about Scripture is that it unveils with ruthless honesty the sins of people who are among its best-known characters. Abraham, Jacob, Moses, David, Hezekiah, Peter, Thomas, James, John, and the rest of the disciples were not morally flawless individuals. They were people like ourselves, who made ghastly mistakes and whose sins were not always in ignorance. The Bible relates the story of the sinner's rebellion, exposure, guilt, repentance, forgiveness and peace. It was by tracing the mercy of God to others that Bunyan dared to believe that he too might be pardoned. Like him, we need the Bible in our everyday life to see how merciful God has been and continues to be to those who seek his mercy and help.

Moreover, Bunyan came to understand something infinitely superior to the example of others. As he read the Scripture for himself, he realised that these characters had cast themselves on the promises of God. He was encouraged by their experience but captivated by God's faithfulness. The promises that appealed to them rang in his own ears. Our daily reading of Scripture and unhurried meditation on its truth will admit us also to the inexhaustible storehouse of God's promises. Here is treasure indeed. Here are not simply demands about what we must do for God, but pledges about what he does for us. Here are described his gifts, resources, sufficiency and liberality.

If we decide to set down in writing the details of our ongoing spiritual pilgrimage, the story of God's promises in our lives ought to have prominence. We are what we are because God has done what he has said. Some magnificent Old Testament words, found in an unusual context, are both an inspiration and a challenge: "God is not a man . . . that he should change his mind. . . . Does he promise and not fulfil?" (Num 23:19). In our allocated daily time for Bible reading and prayer, why not find a biblical promise as often as we can, write it down and then take special notice of particular instances of how God has kept his word? We can never exhaust this mine of riches.

The Encouragement of Friends

Although Bunyan had access to a Bible from his earliest years, the word of God first became persuasive when he heard it from the lips of committed believers. He claimed that until that day, entirely ignorant of Christ, he did everything possible to establish his own righteousness. The corporate testimony of a small group of

Christian women changed all that and initiated his serious pursuit of new life in Christ.

At that time he was fascinated by religious topics and moved closer to these women so that he might overhear, even share, their conversation. The witness of those women was crucial. There were times when Bunyan's quest for faith was harrowing in the extreme, yet through it all he valued beyond words the supportive love of those Bedford believers. When he looked back on this initial experience, he came to see that clear advantages had emerged from his prolonged anguish and later, as a leader caring for others, he took pains to enumerate them. There were at least six ways those women and their fellow members were used to help a seeker in need of Christ.

First, he was impressed by their verbal testimony. He met those "three or four poor women sitting at a door in the sun" as they were "talking about the things of God." He heard the words they spoke but had no understanding of their message. Their "talk was about a new birth, the work of God on their hearts." The women spoke honestly of their earlier unbelief and how impossible it had been to make themselves righteous by their religious practices or moral efforts. Given the importance of such confession of need, the women did not only talk about failure, but they also gloried in the fact that Christ had dealt with their lives.

Bunyan was impressed that they spoke "with such pleasantness of Scripture language, and with such appearance of grace in all they said." They were to him "as if they had found a new world."[35] Their testimony to the grace of God in their lives had an immediate effect upon him; for the first time it exposed his erroneous ideas about being a Christian. Bunyan longed to discover their new world. As he reflected on that transforming encounter, four characteristics of the women's testimony made their appeal: They spoke with assurance, authority, realism and compulsion.

They spoke with assurance. They knew Jesus personally, for they "talked of how God had visited their souls with his love in the Lord Jesus, and with what words and promises they had been refreshed."

They spoke with authority. They did not simply share what

had happened to them, but what could happen to others. They told
Bunyan about particular biblical verses that had supported them.
Their authority was not restricted to what had happened in their
experience, but was written in God's word for everyone. They
pointed beyond themselves to the book that had transformed their
lives.

They spoke with realism. They did not pretend that once they
became Christians, everything worked out splendidly. They talked
openly of fierce conflicts and told him about "the suggestions and
temptations of Satan" and the many subtle ways by which the devil
had tried to undermine their newfound faith. They said nothing to
suggest that it was easy to be a Christian, but they could speak of
"how they were borne up under his assaults" and received strength
beyond their own.

They spoke with compulsion. As Bunyan looked into their radiant faces and listened to their artless conversation, something tugged
at his soul. What impressed him most deeply was that these women
had "such appearance of grace" in all that they said. They shared their
experience of Christ "as if joy did make them speak," and though he
went on his way, "their talk and discourse" went with him.

The memory of those moments never left him. As Bunyan
unfolds the account of his pilgrimage, this segment of the story, the
conversation of those women, is presented as a model of attractive
and effective evangelism.

Secondly, he was challenged by their radical lifestyle. Within
weeks he was meeting those women and their fellow members in the
Bedford Independent Church, and found he could not stay away.
There was something special about them, and it was not simply the
way they talked but the lives they lived. Arrested by their distinctive
and Christlike behaviour, he felt that "they walked like a people who
carried the broad seal of heaven" about them, and he longed to
belong to their number. Although they endeavoured to live at their
best for Christ in everyday life, their hearts were set on heaven.

It seemed to him that they lived "on the sunny side of some
high mountain" whereas he was "shivering and shrinking in the

cold, afflicted with frost, snow and dark clouds," and that although he tried to go to where they were, he was prevented by a wall that kept him in the cold. There was a gap in the wall, "very straight and narrow," and as he reflected on this imaginative picture, he was persuaded that the way to the brighter side of the mountain was through the doorway of personal faith in Christ.[36]

The message had radical implications; entering through that gap in the wall demanded total allegiance to Christ. He alone could not believe, but God used the example of genuine Christians to create that deep longing for personal faith.

Amid the secularism, materialism and pluralism of late twentieth-century society, we might ask how convincingly Christian our personal lifestyle is and whether it has persuasive evangelistic influence. Or as Sangster phrased it in a devastating question: "Are some people outside the church of Christ because I am inside it?"

Thirdly, Bunyan was supported by their hospitality. Those Bedford Christians did everything possible to help him find peace in Christ. They quickly introduced him to their pastor, John Gifford, a man willing to give time to Bunyan in personal conversation and warm-hearted encouragement. Gifford did not merely welcome him to church services but invited him to his home. Bunyan had begun "to look into the Bible with new eyes."[37] There were questions demanding an answer and agonising temptations he needed to discuss with an experienced friend. Gifford appears to have opened his home for small-group discussion, for on these occasions Bunyan could hear the pastor "confer with others about the dealings of God with the soul."[38]

Throughout Christian history men and women have opened their homes to people in need. The early Christians met in homes initially, and across the centuries thousands of seekers have found Christ within the warm hospitality of an open home. All around the world, homes are still being used to express love, promote evangelism, ease loneliness, stimulate prayer, encourage study, deepen fellowship and share burdens. Perhaps as we meditate on Bunyan's indebtedness to his pastor's hospitality, we might quietly reflect on further ways we might use our homes for Christ.

Fourthly, Bunyan was comforted by their genuine love. It was not only the pastor who helped Bunyan. The members of the congregation had also taken him to their hearts, for they soon realised that faith might not come easily to him. He had many struggles before he found peace and assurance, and during those long months they kept alongside him and endeavoured to give him as much help as they could. He says that when he told them of his fierce temptations, doubts and fears, "they would pity me and tell me of the promises."[39]

Helping Bunyan through such extended trials demanded a fair amount of patience and skill. There must have been times when they were almost exasperated by his recurrent phobias and introspective torments. When he looks back on it all, he admits that some of his harrowing thoughts might "seem ridiculous to others,"[40] although they were real enough to him. At times his sense of overwhelming guilt had physical repercussions: "I felt also such a clogging and heat at my stomach by reason of this my terror . . . as if my breast bone would have split in sunder."[41] It was a good thing that the Bedford church had within its membership people who could understand his anguish, absorb his peculiarities and extend to his wounded spirit the necessary love and forbearance.

Not that every Christian helped him in that way. He tells how in great mental turmoil, he once shared with someone the dreadful fear that he had committed the unpardonable sin, only to be told by the man that "he thought so too." It was not the reply to bring peace to a tortured soul: "Here therefore I had but cold comfort."[42] It requires great sensitivity and tenderness, as well as a good knowledge of Scripture, to help people find their way through a spiritual labyrinth of this kind. We cannot hope to know all the answers, so we need great wisdom about how best to respond to people in distress. But we can all show love—and must.

Fifthly, Bunyan was inspired by their knowledge of Scripture. He noticed their delight that God had given so many promises in the Bible and longed that he might claim such truths as his own. John Gifford's great contribution to Bunyan's spiritual pilgrimage was to show him that those who desire faith must not simply sit in the pew, passively accepting teaching from the pulpit merely because the preacher said it. The truth must not only be heard but received and welcomed, made our own, and confirmed by the Holy Spirit as God's special word for us. Gifford encouraged his congregation to believe that there was something more to faith than knowing the great texts of the Bible so that they had a purely intellectual assent to biblical truth. Scriptural promises must become personally effective for them as individuals.

Gifford's faithful preaching gave Bunyan an appetite for the biblical message and urged him not to take up "any truth upon trust," however persuasive the preacher might be. He must seek "evidence from heaven," the inner witness of the Holy Spirit, that a truth in Scripture was not only valid and urgent, but could be applied immediately to his own need. He must "cry mightily to God that he would convince" him of the reality of that word[43] and cry he did. Gifford's plea encouraged him to search the Scriptures, not as a casual enquirer but as a hungry pauper desperate for food. He must search with a new dependence on the Spirit's work to show him where the food was and how he could possess it for himself. The food described, illustrated, and offered in Scripture was to be found in Christ alone, the bread and water of life itself.

Finally, he was sustained by their believing prayer. He had noticed that these believers did not simply talk to each other about spiritual things; on meeting together they had deep and sustained conversations with God. Knowing their commitment to the ministry of intercession, it was natural for Bunyan to seek their help. When he began to experience conviction of sin and great anguish of mind, he desired "the prayers of the people of God,"[44] certain that they would pray for him regularly, sensitively and confidently.

Bunyan's dependence on the prayers of those Bedford believers reminds us of the vital ministry of intercession. We are all far more indebted to the prayers of others than ever we realise, and that assurance ought to inspire us to pray regularly for other people. All too easily our prayers can become narrowly focused on our personal affairs, our homes, families, close friends, local church. For prayer lives to be vibrant, effective and healthy, they need wider horizons. Every Christian ought regularly to carry into the presence of God the needs of other people and do so intelligently by obtaining up-to-date information about the needs of, say, missionary friends, who look to us to give them prayerful support as they work for Christ in countries and cultures different from our own.

Christian Books

Bunyan was not only helped by his contemporaries but by his Christian predecessors. The Bible was the most important book in his life, but other books came to have special significance and were important enough for him to mention in his spiritual autobiography. They remind us that there are vast written resources from the past to encourage our present commitment and aid our growth to maturity.

His first wife, whom he married in 1649, had a godly father, and though the man had died before their wedding, she spoke warmly of his personal holiness. The newly married couple had few possessions, but among them were two books this older Christian had given to his daughter: Arthur Dent's *Plain Man's Pathway to Heaven* and Lewis Bayly's *The Practice of Piety*.

The first, with its imagery of the Christian's journey, may have set Bunyan thinking about the pilgrimage theme that he was to develop later in his famous allegory. If he read it carefully, it confronted him with the challenge of the gospel. Two specific themes in Arthur Dent's book may have addressed Bunyan's sensitive conscience—God's law and the Christian's conflict.

Dent insists on the importance of the law of God, particularly the commandments and their "inwardness," that they address our motives and desires, not simply our actions. It was an important theme with the English Puritan tradition. The point was driven home by special reference to the tenth commandment with its exposure of covetousness, a sin of the heart and mind, not visibly detected by the outward eye. That sensitivity to inward sin certainly stayed with Bunyan.

The second theme from Dent's book helped Bunyan to see that, though completely forgiven, the Christian believer always has to fight against sin. There is no experience of grace that removes the necessity for combat, for "the new creature, or new work of grace, can never be fully fashioned in this life but is always in fashioning."[45]

The other book Bunyan's wife brought as her marriage portion was Lewis Bayly's *The Practice of Piety*. Bayly became Bishop of Bangor, and his book enjoyed considerable popularity in the seventeenth century. It was not, like Dent's, in the form of popular fiction, but was a straightforward devotional book, also written from a decidedly Calvinist perspective. It may have been in this book that Bunyan first read about what became known as "occasional meditation," that is, the idea of using everyday things of life to remind us of spiritual realities, and so meditating on them that the truths they convey become more deeply impressed upon our minds. It was a devotional practice the English Puritans developed in the seventeenth century, and Bayly introduced it as a suggestion for the believer's spiritual life: Going to bed at night reminds the weary of his final sleep; the act of rising in the morning anticipates the resurrection. The morning cock-crow recalls the denial of an overconfident disciple; the bright sunlight, the Son of Righteousness with healing in his wings.[46]

Bunyan makes use of "occasional meditation" in *Grace Abounding*. One day, overwhelmed by his sins, he walked through a field, reflecting on his sad condition. That verse from 1 John 1:7 "took hold" of him: "The blood of Jesus Christ, his Son, cleanses us from all sin." He thought that his sin "when compared to the blood of Christ, was no more than this little clod or stone before me is to this vast and wide field that here I see."[47]

Bunyan says that although these two books did not in his case lead him directly to personal faith, they helped to create a serious interest in spiritual things and were part of an extended process that gradually brought him to an awareness of need. His reference to those particular books alerts us to the fact that we too might use good Christian literature to awaken a desire among our unbelieving friends, neighbours and work colleagues for the things that matter most of all. This kind of activity is a form of pre-evangelism. It prepares the way for the reception of the gospel. Many people in our own time have been grateful that similar books were loaned to them, by writers like C. S. Lewis, covering some of the intellectual difficulties that appear as huge stumbling blocks to our contemporaries.

A more influential book in Bunyan's life was Luther's commentary on Galatians, which he regarded as God's special gift to him at an extremely difficult time. Troubled that he was guilty of blasphemy and might not be forgiven, he yearned for some message of comfort and hope. He had looked for some time for a book, possibly written before he was born, so that from "some ancient godly man's experience" he might draw deeply. The copy of Luther's commentary that came into his hands was almost falling to pieces, but after only turning a few of its frail pages, he says he found his condition described in Luther's experience "as if his book had been written out of my heart." With deep gratitude he acknowledged his debt, saying that, apart from Scripture, he preferred Luther's book more than all the books he had ever seen, "as most fit for a wounded conscience."[48]

In that book Luther's experience crossed the barriers of time and culture. The Reformer's interpretation of a New Testament letter and the sharing of his personal experience spanned the centuries and reached a man of totally different context, social background, educational advantage and intellectual ability. The reading of good books can make a highly creative contribution to our spiritual development, especially if we find unhurried time to read some of those written by outstanding Christians over the centuries. Richard Baxter was greatly influenced as a teenager by reading his father's copy of

Richard Sibbes's *Bruised Reed*. William Wilberforce was indebted to Philip Doddridge for his *Rise and Progress of Religion in the Soul*. Many of our contemporaries have been helped by the introduction to some of the great Christian classics in Richard J. Foster and James Bryan Smith, *Devotional Classics*.[49] There are a number of reasons why the reading of such books can enrich our spirituality.

First, they widen our horizons. We are all in danger of being "locked in" to those theological ideas and emphases that have become popular in our own generation. We may blandly accept that these contemporary Christian topics are of primary importance—and they may not be. The dominant aspects of a fashionable modern message may need to be balanced by complementary biblical truths. Other generations of writers help us to gain that necessary perspective about Christian teaching. It is not easy for the limited confines of the human mind to hold in perfect balance the entire range of Christian truth. Some of the characteristic emphases of our own day may not necessarily be the whole of the truth. There are "blind spots" in our thinking, and omissions in contemporary Christian teaching may be exposed by reading books from earlier periods of Christian history.

Secondly, great Christian writers of earlier generations help us to evaluate our priorities. We imagine that the ways we plan and express our Christian devotion, work and witness are the best and most effective, and that may not necessarily be so. Believers from other centuries have also experienced close communion with God, identification with Christ, and the inspiration of the Holy Spirit, just as much as we have—perhaps more so. What they shared about their personal and corporate discoveries was not intended solely for their contemporaries. If we hold some truth particularly dear, we never imagine that its value is restricted to our limited lifetime. We want it to be handed on to the next generation. If it has transformed, encouraged, refined and sustained us, we naturally hope that our children and grandchildren will also benefit by it. So, likewise, when our forefathers took the trouble to put their best thoughts in writing, they too hoped that it might be of help to their children and later generations who might have access to their books. It is arrogant to imagine that they have nothing to say to us.

Thirdly, writers of earlier generations help to enrich our devotion. They discovered through their own experience of prayer and meditation some helpful dimensions of personal spirituality that inspired their adoration, petition and intercession. The way they expressed their love for God cannot possibly be a matter of indifference to their spiritual successors. It is a privilege to be known as a disciple of Christ; the name means "learner." If we are willing to learn from our contemporaries, why not also from our predecessors?

Fourthly, they challenge our commitment. Reading their story, we are likely to find ourselves admiring their heroism, fortitude, patience and love. They belong to the great "cloud of witnesses" (Heb 12:1-2) who testify to the faithfulness and generosity of God and whose example cheers us on in the race set before us.

Fifthly, they increase our confidence. If God could see them through some of the immense trials and hazards they encountered and enable them to cope creatively with massive personal disadvantages, we may become more deeply persuaded that the God who sustained them will not disappoint us.

Inspired Preaching

In his acute spiritual distress, Bunyan was helped not only by reading Luther's exposition but also by listening to good contemporary preaching. He provides us with a fascinating example of how one seventeenth-century preacher interpreted an Old Testament text. Bunyan recalls a sermon he heard when, oppressed with guilt, he thought that everyone in the world had a far better heart than he had, and that for "inward wickedness and pollution of mind" he was as bad as the devil himself. Yet "when comforting time was come," a preacher announced a text from the Song of Solomon (4:1): "Behold thou art fair my love," concentrating on those two closing words, *my love*. The preacher developed his theme under five headings: that

Christ's love is for the church (often unloved by others), that his love is totally undeserved, that Christ loved although he was so bitterly hated, that Christ loves us even when we fear he does not, and that nothing in life is more important than the love of Christ.

Bunyan says he was not particularly gripped by what was being said until the preacher arrived at his fourth point. He sat up when the man urged that those who were "under temptation to desertion" should remember that "the saved soul is Christ's love."

> Then poor tempted soul, when you are assaulted and afflicted with temptation, and the hiding of God's face, yet think on those two words, *my love*, still.

As Bunyan walked home, those two words were captivating, and enabled him at that time to look away from his tormenting thoughts to the Lord who loved him still. His dejected spirit was lifted by the preacher's message of strong assurance.

> Then I began to give place to the Word, which with power, did over and over make this joyful sound within my soul, *Thou art my Love* . . . and nothing shall separate you from my love.

In communicating his message of the love of Christ, the preacher had done some excellent things. He had taken one aspect of an immense biblical doctrine rather than devote his time to issues of peripheral importance. He had exalted Christ. He had concentrated his message into one short unforgettable phrase so that his attractive theme could be easily recalled. He had addressed a recurrent pastoral issue by preaching sympathetically to people who, in the light of current experience, might be tempted to doubt the love of Christ. He had offered practical help as to how they might cope with such a condition. It had impressed one man so deeply that he wanted to tell everybody about it. We do not know the name of the preacher, but Bunyan never forgot the sermon. Like the conversation with the women, it played a significant part in pointing him directly to Christ.

Bunyan's long pilgrimage went on, but for that day's preaching, the gratitude was euphoric. Such truth must be shared: "I thought I could have spoken of his love, and of his mercy to me, even to the very crows that sat upon the ploughed lands before me."[50]

SHARING GOD'S GRACE

As Bunyan draws toward the close of his book, his deep pastoral concern is given greater expression. He hopes that his story might have persuasive evangelistic appeal, convincing the unbeliever of the seriousness of sin and the miracle of grace, but primarily he writes for Christians. His "fatherly care and desire" for their spiritual welfare[51] becomes specific about ways in which his spiritual afflictions and physical imprisonment have brought enriching dimensions to his spiritual life. Despite all the pain and anguish, he says he "would not have been without this trial for much," and writes with gratitude about the teaching he has had by it.[52] He has meditated long on these "spoils won in battle," and writes that other Christians might benefit from his experience and so be helped to build themselves up spiritually. Perhaps when we go through difficult times, it could be helpful for us to reflect on the grace that has come to us and the light that has shone in the darkness. Thinking about such things enables us to discern that God's best gifts may come to us when everything else seems against us. Such "songs in the night" ought not to be lost but set down in writing as the result of our own meditation and as a testimony to the help we have certainly received. When Bunyan records his story, five great themes emerge in his meditation on the blessings that come to a believer through adversity. They have spoken persuasively to him about God, Christ, sin, the Bible and heaven.

The Holiness of God

Bunyan is convinced that trials such as his can be used to heighten our awareness of the transcendent holiness of God. Reflecting on those agonizing months when he feared he had rejected Christ, he wants to share the advantages he has "gained by this temptation . . . By this I was made continually to possess in my soul a very wonderful sense of the being and glory of God." Thus, though his initial encounter with God was "in a way of exceeding dread and terror," it saved him from trivialising spiritual realities as he had done at one time.[53] While he was pleased with his modest religious and moral achievements, he thought he could earn God's favour, but an uncomfortable awareness of the character of God became the first step of his spiritual pilgrimage. Reverence was vital; nobody can begin to have the least understanding of the privilege and responsibility of Christian living without some perception of the divine majesty.

The Sufficiency of Christ

Even as he struggled with the fear that he had turned Christ away from his life, Bunyan realised, as the painful months went by, how deep was his need of Christ—an essential foundation for every Christian. Any experience that increases our sense of dependence on Christ must be regarded as working for our good.

As we have seen, it was only very slowly that Bunyan came to appropriate the promise of Christ, that "him that cometh to me I will in no wise cast out" (Jn 6:37). But once he had done so, the unshakeable steadfastness of Christ's love was a living truth to him, which he appreciated all the more after his long battle.

Ultimately, even the crushing sense of guilt was revealed as an expression of God's mercy: It is the route by which prodigals return home, and it was by travelling this road that Bunyan arrived at the place where he could gratefully place his trust in the Son of God.

During his lonely imprisonment, he was comforted by a deeper experience of Christ: "Jesus Christ also was never more real and apparent than now; here I have seen him and felt him indeed."[54] In adversity his love for and appreciation of Christ were strengthened,

and Christ himself was established more and more firmly at the
centre of his life.

> Of all tears, they are the best that are made by the blood of
> Christ; and of all joy, that is the sweetest that is mixed with
> mourning over Christ. O 'tis a goodly thing to be on our
> knees, with Christ in our arms, before God.[55]

The Seriousness of Sin

Bunyan's trials and his acute awareness of sin saved him from a
superficial estimate of human failure and enabled him to see the
waywardness of his own heart. However, his sense of sin was not
confined to the earliest stages of his pilgrimage, soon to be dis-
carded as a remote item of spiritual autobiography.

Even as he writes his conclusion, he acknowledges that, for all
his deep experience of God, he must still struggle against ingratitude
and coldness in prayer. As a mature believer, he sees that although
the continued presence of sin in his heart causes him great distress,
this, in the wisdom of God, works for his good. His painful consciousness of sin forces him to mistrust his own abilities; it drives him
to pray more earnestly and to look to God, through Christ, to help
him through the trials and temptations of this life. Realistic awareness of sin is a vital component of a healthy spiritual life.

The Resources of God's Word

In adversity Bunyan made a further discovery; he came to appreciate the unlimited resources of God's word. The ultimate result of
his prolonged battle with doubt and despair was a grateful trust in
the promises of Scripture, and he emerged as a pauper who had
stumbled across incalculable wealth. "The Scriptures now also
were wonderful things unto me. I saw that the truth and verity of
them were the keys of the kingdom of heaven."

Later, his years of imprisonment increased his love for the

Bible. Within its pages he began to value things he had hardly seen before. From his cell he could write:

> I have never had in all my life so great an inlet into the word of God as now; Scriptures that I saw nothing in before are made in this place and state to shine upon me.

When he felt bereft and lonely, isolated from wife, family and fellow Christians, then God's word became his companion and friend and "with one Scripture and another" strengthened him against everything that would daunt his spirit.[56]

After the resolution of his great crisis of doubt, Bunyan was never again subject to such prolonged despair. But he was not, of course, immune to the perils of despondency that all Christians may experience from time to time. The strain of his long ordeal had weakened his health, and he suffered several bouts of serious illness; he found that at such times, when a believer has to face the prospect of death, the devil is particularly active in seeking to deceive him concerning his eternal security. It is in connection with this experience that we will begin to look at one final "spoil won in battle."

The Assurance of Heaven

It was Bunyan's practice to keep his hope of heaven constantly before his eyes, and naturally this was especially so when he was so ill that death seemed imminent. He set himself to reflect on God's promises—but immediately his mind was so filled with the recollection of his failings that his hope vanished, and he was possessed by a great fear of death. Once more the grace of God reached down and lifted him up, assuring him that "not by works of righteousness that we have done but according to his mercy he hath saved us" (Titus 3:5). Fear left him: "now death was lovely and beautiful in my sight, for I saw we shall never live indeed till we be gone to the other world."[57]

This was a genuine experience of certainty concerning the hope of heaven, but we must always beware of concluding prematurely that the conflict is finally resolved or the lesson finally learned. Further battles lay ahead in prison.

When he was first imprisoned, Bunyan feared (though the fear was without foundation) that he might be hanged. Confronted by the prospect of this terrible death, he was overwhelmed once more by his unworthiness and by fear of dying. His prayers for comfort and strength to face the ordeal went unanswered; God seemed utterly absent. For several weeks he wrestled with the fear that he would be lost.

Finally, he looked his worst fear squarely in the face: If he should be lost, what then? He realised that his duty to hold fast to the "word and way of God" remained unchanged. He concluded that "it was my duty to stand to his word whether he would ever look on me or no, or save me at the last." Then he remembered Satan's charge that Job's faithfulness to God was worth nothing if it depended on the benefits he had received. So too Bunyan's own obligation to serve God could not be conditional on any blessing to be had for his faithfulness—even if heaven itself were to be denied him, he could not go back on the commitment he had professed.

> I am for going on, and venturing my eternal state with Christ, whether I have comfort here or no. . . . I will leap off the ladder even blindfolded into eternity, sink or swim, come heaven, come hell. Lord Jesus, if you will catch me, do; if not, I will venture for your name.[58]

This resolve in itself brought him great comfort by reassuring him that his allegiance to God was genuine. But it also demonstrated one of the great paradoxes of the Christian life: It is to those who desire to serve God for his own sake, and not solely for the sake of a heavenly reward, that the certainty of heaven is increased. Having thus determined to serve God without thought of any reward, Bunyan subsequently found that his former assurance returned with even greater force, and he was granted a foretaste of the joy of being with Christ: "I have had sweet sights of . . . my being with Jesus in another world. . . . I have seen that here, that I am persuaded I shall never, while in this world, be able to express."[59] Truly a "spoil won from battle."

Bunyan shares his experiences of God's grace to testify to the blessings that came when he was "afflicted and oppressed." Adversity is not profitless if it leads us nearer to God, makes us more aware of our dependence on him and better equips us for service in the world.

The honesty and realism of Bunyan speak powerfully to us still. A compassionate God like ours ensures that, however deep the valleys, pilgrims are brought safely home. Over the centuries the Lord has never disappointed his people. Whatever the hardships, Bunyan was assured of unfailing help—and so are we.

.✝.

JOHN WESLEY

Journal

Freely to All
Ourselves We Give

The eighteenth century produced some outstandingly gifted people, and Wesley may have been the most energetic of them all. He lived longer than most of his contemporaries, and his years (1703-91) spanned the century. After a brief biographical sketch, we shall look at his famous journal and see how graphically it illustrates Christian qualities and gifts, so that we might discern its message for ourselves.

HIS LIFE

When John Wesley told a fellow leader, "Were I ... to write my own life, I should begin it before I was born,"[1] he was acknowledging a debt to godly parents and grandparents. Wesley was born into the family of an impulsive, impractical but devout Lincolnshire clergyman. Samuel Wesley owed his education to the influential Dissenting academies, but from his years at two of the best of them, he emerged a convinced member of the Church of England. He married another devout Anglican with nonconformist ancestry, Susannah Annesley, who was probably the greatest influence on their many children. John was the fifteenth child, and the Epworth home was not without its hardships; during childhood there was "little but bread to eat, and not great plenty of that."[2] Through little fault of his own, Samuel Wesley was not a popular rector. John always maintained that their home was deliberately set on fire by hostile neighbours, and it was from an upper room window that as a five-year-old boy he was lifted from the flames. Throughout life he viewed the rescue as a miraculous intervention, believing that, as "a brand plucked from the burning," he was destined to serve God and his contemporaries.

For his formal education John went to Charterhouse and then to Oxford, where he was later elected to a fellowship at Lincoln College. During his university years he became a leader among a group that met regularly for reading, spiritual inspiration, mutual correction and prison visitation. It became known among critics as the "Holy Club," and because of their strictly disciplined pattern of life, its members were dubbed "Methodists." Several other members, as well as John, later became leading personalities in the eighteenth-century religious scene, such as John's brother Charles, George Whitefield—the revival's most gifted preacher—and the popular devotional writer, James Hervey.

John Wesley served for a brief period as his father's curate, but in 1735 he and Charles sailed for Georgia to be chaplains to colonists and hopefully to serve as missionaries among the local Indians. During the outward journey, their ship encountered fierce storms. Afraid of death, John was impressed by the calm trust and spirituality of some fellow passengers who were Moravians, a continental Protestant group of Lutheran stock, a people of warm personal devotion and active missionary commitment.

His years in Georgia were far from happy, and within three years he had returned home, bewildered and despondent, searching for a deeper faith. Back in London, his Moravian contacts led to a memorable spiritual experience on 24 May 1738. That night, "very unwillingly," he went to a meeting house in Aldersgate Street where, as he listened to a reading from Luther's preface to the Letter to the Romans, he felt his "heart strangely warmed." As he heard Luther's words describing "the change which God works in the heart through faith in Christ," the certainty came:

I felt I did trust in Christ, Christ alone for salvation; and an assurance was given me that he had taken away *my* sins, even *mine*, and saved *me* from the law of sin and death.[3]

Also influenced by the Moravians, his younger brother Charles had been brought to clear faith and assurance three days earlier, largely through reading Luther on Galatians. The two brothers were to become outstanding leaders of the evangelical revival in England. John was the effective evangelist, author and organiser, while Charles, in addition to being a prolific hymn-writer, was also minister for over twenty years among the Methodist people in Bristol, before devoting his last seventeen years to the care of their London congregation.

In the decades that followed their conversion, both men travelled enormous distances, though John's journeys on horseback were more extensive, including regular visits to Scotland, Wales and Ireland. His travels, about 8,000 miles a year, covered a triangular circuit between the three main centres of Methodist influence in London, Newcastle and Bristol. This determined itinerant ministry involved regular visitation of established Methodist societies of believers for teaching and pastoral care as well as fervent evangelistic preaching to crowds that were frequently vast and, at times, unruly and hostile.

The incessant travels were inspired by the deep theological conviction that Christ's saving death must be preached to all. Vigorously opposed to any suggestion that the possibility of salvation was limited to a favoured few, Wesley used every opportunity, through preaching, personal conversation and writing (books and letters) to share his three main convictions. He believed that, first, everybody *can* be saved (unlimited redemption); secondly, they can *know* that they are saved (Christian assurance); and, thirdly, they are saved from *all* sin—his doctrine of holiness, or "perfect love" as he preferred to describe it.

His dedicated and vigorous leadership meant that by the time of his death he had enlisted the partnership of at least 300 preachers and gathered a membership of over 70,000 followers in Great Britain, to say nothing of his colleagues and society members in missionary work overseas, particularly in America.

His success owed much to his godly upbringing, rigourous discipline, strong physique, organisational skill, wide reading, firm convictions, generous spirit and the ability to recruit new partners for the work, discerning and encouraging their different gifts.

Although he grasped every opportunity to preach outdoors, he was a great lover of order, reverence and dignity, and said he greatly preferred an attentive congregation gathered in a local church with its neat pews, elevated pulpit and large Bible on its velvet cushion. Daily contact with people of all kinds confirmed his belief that evangelistic preaching was not optional, but a matter of urgent necessity. Once converts were won, they became members of local Methodist societies, supporting each other by weekly meetings for prayer, Bible study, spiritual fellowship and practical help. To follow his itinerary with the aid of the *Journal* is to be in the presence of a man who was always pressing on to the next assignment, using every moment to serve Christ through his many gifts.

Wesley's ministry as a travelling evangelist was a phenomenal achievement even from a physical perspective, to say nothing of its emotional, intellectual and spiritual demands. Augustine Birrell compared it to a parliamentary election campaign, worthy of a potential member's undivided effort for about three weeks, but leaving most candidates totally exhausted at the end.[4] Wesley maintained that relentless pace, speaking in the open air several times a day, for over fifty years, travelling about a quarter of a million miles and preaching over 40,000 sermons. When old age made travel impossible, he gave himself unsparingly to the work in London. In his early eighties he was visiting prosperous homes in London, trudging through the melting snow, collecting two hundred pounds to buy clothes for the poor during a hard winter.

Among his extensive writings, the *Journal* was certainly the most popular, and we look now at its origin, nature and purpose.

HIS BOOK

Wesley believed it was impossible to cultivate an effective Christian life without firm disciplined structures. His mother was probably the first to inculcate in his young mind the belief that idleness was at the root of most sins and that in order to avoid it, believers should make themselves accountable for every hour. The idea of a carefully planned day with fixed times for prayer, Bible reading, meditation, instruction of children and servants, diligent work and service for others had its origins in English Puritanism, and was developed by several seventeenth-century Christian writers. Jeremy Taylor's words in *Holy Living and Holy Dying* about taking "an exact account of the manner in which time is spent" inspired Wesley to start keeping a personal diary to record and check "the manner wherein I spent my time, writing down how I had employed every hour." Unless the day was meticulously organised and given appropriate balance, irreplaceable hours could be wasted and lost.

His hardworking, spiritually devout mother only maintained her large family by adopting a timetable, and from their earliest days the Wesley children knew what it was to live according to rule. By the time Wesley reached Oxford, his normal working day had assumed a definite structure, and his daily diary helped him to live responsibly as a man accountable to God for every hour. The diary was not intended for publication but began as a personal record kept in order to check this self-imposed pattern of disciplined living.

Jeremy Taylor said that holiness of life could be encouraged if "before we sleep each night, we examine the actions of the past day with a particular scrutiny." Wesley did precisely that with scrupulous care, rising early throughout his long life, giving every available hour to the work of God.

The diary entries were made in abbreviated writing, complicated cipher or shorthand, but in 1735 his travels in Georgia encouraged him to prepare separately for publication a journal that would naturally include some information found in the diary but would be supplemented by additional material about places he visited and the people he met. The published *Journal* was intended to encourage the societies and, at the same time, reach the frequently critical non-Methodist reader. As the *Journal* continued to be published in its twenty-one parts, Wesley deliberately included a selection of events likely to interest and edify all his readers, Christians and unbelievers alike.

The *Journal* was consistently useful in the practical encouragement it offered to the societies. Scattered over a wide area, his people had limited opportunity to meet with other Methodists and to learn from each other how the work was progressing elsewhere, what experiments others had adopted in the work of evangelism and how they had coped with pastoral difficulties and local opposition. Every few years, therefore, instalments of the journal were eagerly purchased by Methodist believers all over the country who were keen to learn both of their leader's experiences and about the ordinary members whose conversion, spiritual progress, service and influence he was pleased to relate in considerable detail.

Wesley also selected his material with opponents in mind. Methodism had many enemies, and he was personally exposed to endless criticism. Few of his months were free from some kind of defamation and abuse. Leaflets were frequently published denigrating the Methodists and slandering their leader.[5] Members of the societies, especially their preachers, were constantly vilified. Although Wesley recognised that some persecution was inevitable in the Christian life, he believed it was important for the English-reading public to know how he was spending his time, where he had been in his travels and what the Methodists were doing in their meetings and for the communities they served. For this reason, the *Journal* consistently records the message of the preacher, relates stories of personal conversions and describes the reaction of the crowds, whether they were responsive, hostile or indifferent to the preaching of the gospel.

The man who published his famous *Journal* was not without faults. He once said that Luther might have been a better man if his friends had been more critical of his unbridled speech and occasionally erratic conduct.[6] It is fair comment, though, that now and again Wesley might also have benefited from a word of gentle correction from one of his many appreciative colleagues. Yet for all the obvious failings, he was head and shoulders above most of his believing contemporaries and certainly one of the most remarkable Christians of all time. Enviable qualities far outweigh his foibles. We turn now to look at some of the great themes in the *Journal*, not only to understand the influence of his magnetic personality but also to derive help and inspiration for our own Christian lives.

HIS MESSAGE

If we had to choose one word to summarise the message of the Wesleys, it would have to be "love." Love is a recurrent rhapsody in Charles Wesley's hymns and a dominant note in John Wesley's preaching and teaching. As we look at the *Journal*, we shall trace the theme in the four aspects that were given special prominence in their ministry—love for the Lord, love for the lost, love for the believers and love for the unloved.

Love for God—the Quest for Holiness

Once the early Methodist people were brought to personal faith in Christ, they were urged to pursue holiness. Wesley used a number of terms to describe this experience of the Christian ideal—"second blessing,"[7] "full salvation,"[8] and "Christian perfection"[9]—but his preference was for "perfect love,"[10] a phrase drawn from his favourite letter, John's First Epistle. Wesley's encouragement to his people to live each day as men and women utterly devoted to God is found in various different contexts throughout the *Journal*. In one volume he includes a letter that explains what he meant by this further experience of grace.

> I told you it was love; the love of God and our neighbour; the image of God stamped on the heart; the life of God in the soul

of man; the mind that was in Christ, enabling us to walk as Christ also walked.[11]

In a letter to an Anglican minister who was critical of the doctrine, the former slave-trader, John Newton, Wesley explains how he came to formulate and proclaim his holiness message. During his Oxford days he had been struck by the chapter on Intention in Jeremy Taylor's *Holy Living and Holy Dying* and says he "felt a fixed intention to give myself up to God." His later reading of Thomas à Kempis's *Imitation of Christ* further encouraged him to give God all his heart—"That is just what I mean by Perfection now." A year or two later William Law's *Christian Perfection* and *A Serious Call to a Devout and Holy Life* made him "more explicitly resolved to be all devoted to God in body, soul and spirit." He told Newton that all his desire was fully expressed in Gerhardt's hymn that had been translated by Wesley and included in his first hymn book:

> *O grant that nothing in my soul*
> *May dwell, but Thy pure love alone.*
> *O may Thy love possess me whole,*
> *My joy, my treasure, and my crown.*
> *Strange flames far from my heart remove*
> *My every act, word, thought be love.*

To which he added: "And I am still persuaded this is what the Lord Jesus has bought for me with his own blood."[12]

Newton was not the only evangelical to be uneasy about the term "perfection," but, whatever its name, Wesley's holiness teaching seems to focus on two indisputable aspects of the ideal Christian life—surrender to God and Christlikeness. He constantly maintained that such a lifestyle was always attainable by claiming the believer's promised resources in Christ—resources that must be renewed both in daily dependence and total obedience.

Although Wesley asserted that this experience of grace could be received "*now* by simple *faith*,"[13] he did not regard holiness as an isolated crisis or pinnacle of spiritual achievement. His preaching never failed to emphasise the necessity of steady continuance:

> ... and when you have attained a measure of perfect love ...
> think not of resting there. That is impossible. You cannot
> stand still; you must either rise or fall; rise higher or fall
> lower.[14]

Wesley's holiness teaching was not always precisely defined, but his aim was clear enough. He longed for his converts to go on with Christ, and for that reason his message about ideal Christian commitment was presented in essentially practical terms. Although "perfect love" could not be obtained solely by human effort, neither could it be retained without it. He did not believe in effortless Christianity. He recognised that Christian experience was bound at some point or other to involve the believer in conflict situations.

Skilfully weaving his message into the fabric of brilliant story-telling, Wesley uses his *Journal* to make it clear that there is no holiness without sacrifice. Two insidious hazards lurk in the path of every believer—the danger of *pampering* ourselves and of *protecting* ourselves. Two practical implications of his holiness teaching challenge these twin perils; believers need both spiritual discipline and moral courage. Discipline is a component of holiness, and courage is the evidence of holiness.

The first conflict is within. We are frequently confronted with the temptation to *pamper* ourselves. "Perfect love" means that in every situation the believer is resolute about putting surrender to God and love for Christ before personal comfort. It is nothing other than the teaching of Jesus about taking up the cross (Mk 8:34-38), about "losing" our life rather than "keeping" it for ourselves. That means that personal preferences are always subservient to the will of God and the glory of Christ. For Wesley this was not some kind of vague mystical experience. It meant having shape and design for every day. Love for God was more than an emotional sense of gratitude. If God is loved, then we must give priority to the time we spend with him. For Wesley that meant rising early in order to meet unhurriedly with the God he adored.

The *Journal* did not describe his daily activity in order to assure the Methodists that they had an energetic personality at the helm. The pattern of personal devotion and sacrificial living was for imitation not admiration, and it is presented by means of a daily narrative that encourages something more than praise. The members of the societies were being taught that discipline is part of the ongoing experience of every Christian, not just of their admired leader. Holiness of life can only be attained through reliance on Christ and not by good works, but, equally, there is no sanctity without sacrifice.

Every society member knew that before Wesley preached to them, however early in the morning, he had first talked with God. Each day had order, shape and design, and every moment was offered for the service of Christ. Time must never be wasted. If he was riding, then he did so "with a slack rein" so that the time might be used for reading. If illness or an accident prevented him from preaching, then he would use the opportunity for writing. Once he slipped on the ice while crossing London Bridge. He limped to a nearby chapel to preach, "being resolved not to disappoint the people." After the sermon his leg was bound up by a surgeon so that he could walk on to the next engagement. Unable thereafter to get about, he spent the remainder of the week, partly in prayer, reading and conversation, partly in compiling a Hebrew grammar and writing a book for children. On the following Sunday he was still not able to stand so he preached to the London society kneeling, and did so again on two occasions after the weekend.[15]

He was a man of extraordinary stamina. Once in the West country he was afflicted with a violent stomach disorder that gave him a continual headache and cramp in his feet and legs, but he rode on, being unwilling to disappoint the congregation, and preached on "Be careful for nothing."[16] He often put in a day's work when he was sick. On an October Saturday in 1753 he found himself "out of order, but believed it would go off." By the Sunday he "was considerably worse, but could not think of sparing myself on that day." The next day he says that he "rose extremely sick, yet I determined, if it were possible, to keep my word, and accordingly set out soon after four for Canterbury."[17]

Wesley was blessed with indomitable perseverance and resilience. Capable of immense physical exertion, he tackled all his work with eager determination and boundless energy. From its beginning, the *Journal* often mentions his travels through difficult terrain in appalling weather. One winter Sunday he felt "very weak and faint," but the following morning he "rose soon after three, lively and strong" and found all his "complaints were fled away like a dream." It was just as well, for he needed all his strength that day, encountering wind and snow that drove full in his face, only to be followed by large hailstones so sharp and biting that he and his companions could hardly see nor breathe. But, undeterred, he preached early that evening "to a serious congregation."[18]

Reports of that kind are far from rare. Torrential rain sometimes made the roads "so dirty and slippery" that their "horses could hardly keep their feet."[19] He frequently preached in bad weather: "The congregation regarded it no more than I did; though I was thoroughly wet before I had done, the shower driving full in my face."[20] Biting winds, "ready to cut us in two," did not deter him,[21] and stormy crossings were taken in his stride. When the Irish Sea was "boiling like a pot," God "smoothed the face of the deep" and gave them "a small fair wind."[22] Caught once in a flooded area of London, he owed his life to a passing coachman who got him to safety.[23]

His famous *Notes on the New Testament* might never have been written had he "not been so ill as not to be able to preach, and yet so well as to be able to read and write."[24] He was out of the pulpit for four months, but during that time his written work proved to be of immense value to his preachers. He was always thinking of others.

Up early every morning, he could not understand why some people could not attend a preaching service before going to work. On one occasion he delayed preaching until 9 A.M., "for the sake of the tender and delicate ones."[25] The words "resolved" and "determined" are part of the *Journal*'s characteristic vocabulary. They give expression to its writer's commitment to disciplined spirituality. He certainly did not pamper himself.

The second danger for these Christians, especially in a hostile environment, was that of *protecting* themselves. Courage was the evidence of holiness. When a life is devoted to God, "perfect love" will cast out fear. Wesley knew that Methodism was "everywhere spoken against"[26] and responded by saying that Christians who had devoted their lives to God and were committed to Christlike living should neither be surprised by persecution nor afraid of it. Strength would always be given in times of fierce adversity.

In travelling the country, Wesley sought to encourage the societies; in hard times they needed his inspiring support and advice. It was not always easy to maintain their witness. A hostile crowd was easily mobilised in the eighteenth century, and the Methodists had enough opponents around to ensure that the anger of an unruly mob could get seriously out of hand. Antagonism was expressed by a variety of people.

For example, Wesley and his followers were frequently opposed by those appointed to maintain the law. Under the harsh provisions of parliamentary legislation, Dissenters had suffered greatly in the period following 1662, but the Toleration Act of 1689 had given them freedom to worship according to conscience. However, because the Methodists were not Dissenters and claimed mostly to be loyal members of the Church of England, simply meeting in societies for mutual inspiration, they were not always given the liberty they desired for worship and fellowship. When they endeavoured to obtain licences for their buildings, applications were refused, and they were dismissed as lawbreakers. So when a mob hindered the Methodists as they worshipped or attacked Wesley and his companions as they preached outdoors, few magistrates would think of coming to their assistance.

Local gentry were also among the opponents of Methodism, and if they knew that Wesley was in the area, many of these people were quite capable of ensuring that a cruel mob was in the right place at the right time. Although Wesley had many friends among his fellow Anglican ministers, unsympathetic clergymen were also responsible for encouraging local opposition to Wesley's preaching. When a parish priest was also a magistrate, it could be hazardous for local Methodists, especially when one of their leaders visited the district. The Vicar of Wednesbury was irritated when members of his congregation linked up with the local Methodist society; he made the offenders sign to say that "they would never read, or sing, or pray together, or hear the Methodist preachers any more."[27] Failure to comply invited an attack on their property, even the demolition of their homes. Whatever the locality, ordinary employers, neighbours and even family members could create difficulties for Wesley's followers.

Sometimes a violent crowd surrounded a property owned by one of Wesley's followers and destroyed both building and contents. Charles Wesley said it was easy to identify "our people's houses" as he rode through Darlaston because, following earlier troubles, their "windows were all stopped up."[28]

It was particularly dangerous for Staffordshire Methodists during the winter of 1744. One of Wesley's colleagues there wrote to tell him of the sufferings of his friends at Darlaston where a Methodist couple were assaulted by an aggressive mob that was particularly violent with the woman: "Their little children, meantime, as well as themselves, wandered up and down, no one daring to relieve or take them in, lest they should hazard their own lives."

Welcoming a national Methodist leader could be particularly difficult for the locals. It exposed them to the attention of aggressive opponents. Soon after Charles Wesley left Wednesbury during a Staffordshire preaching tour, the mob became increasingly aggressive and

> assaulted, one after another, all the houses of those who were called Methodists. They first broke all their windows . . . all the tables, chairs, chests of drawers, with whatever was not easily removable, they dashed in pieces, particularly shop-

goods, and furniture of every kind. What they could not well break, as feather-beds, they cut in pieces and strewed about the room. . . . All this time none offered to resist them. Indeed, both men and women fled for their lives; only the children stayed, not knowing whither to go.

Crowds could be guilty of appalling physical cruelty as well as wanton destruction; the Wednesbury mob threw a pregnant woman off her bed and then tore it to shreds.

But most of these Methodist people were as resilient as their leaders. Threatened with further trouble, they said, "We have already lost all our goods, and nothing more can follow but the loss of our lives, which we will lose too, rather than wrong our consciences."[29]

In all these experiences societies could count on the sympathetic, prayerful and practical support of their leader. When John Wesley heard of initial persecution in Staffordshire, he was the first to ride north in order to be alongside his suffering friends.[30] Regular issues of the *Journal* enabled others to know how sensitive he was to the needs of his people in trouble.

What inspired a persecuted congregation most was the knowledge that Wesley's sympathy was based on his own frequent experience of adversity. He knew what it was to encounter aggressive individuals and hostile mobs. More than once he used the *Journal* to reflect on how God had protected him in potentially dangerous situations. During the 1743 Staffordshire riots, a vicious crowd was intent on killing him, but when the trouble was over, he only wished to recall "by how gentle degrees does God prepare us for His will!"

Two years ago a piece of brick grazed my shoulders. It was a year after that the stone struck me between the eyes. Last month I received one blow, and this evening two . . . but both were as nothing: for though one man struck me on the breast with all his might, and the other on the mouth with such a force that the blood gushed out immediately, I felt no more pain from either of the blows than if they had touched me with a straw.[31]

Experiences of this kind, frequently recorded in the *Journal*, served to remind its readers that it is not easy to be a Christian. They further emphasised that there is no holiness without suffering. Some experience of rejection plays a vital part in the sanctification of every believer. The Christian who is surrendered to God and determined to follow Christ inevitably walks the way of the cross. At some point or other, that is likely to involve some form of opposition.

In late twentieth-century Western society, Christian faith and witness rarely involve us in physical danger, though many of our fellow Christians in other parts of the world never expect such immunity. But we may well experience other forms of adversity— domestic tension, unpopularity, social isolation, verbal abuse, ostracism, ridicule. Wesley's courageous example alerted the Methodist people to the temptation to protect themselves from such trouble. Heroism and holiness went hand in hand.

Readers of the *Journal* in the contemporary world may well be alerted to areas of apathy, indifference, ease or carelessness in their own lives. Are we entirely guiltless in the matter of pampering ourselves? Is our witness for Christ minimised because of our concern to protect ourselves from opposition or social stigma?

Much of Wesley's own experience of hardship was due to his vigorous evangelistic concern, and we now turn to that crucial aspect of his ministry so graphically portrayed throughout the *Journal*.

Love for the Lost—the Passion for Witness

Wesley and his partners endured suffering not only as an expression of their devotion to God but because of their love for the unconverted. For Wesley, this compassion was given initial expression in passionate evangelistic preaching. The Aldersgate Street experience thrust him out of that Moravian meeting room into a waiting and frequently hostile world. Love drove him on—love for Christ, love for the message, and love for the people. He could not be enclosed within the narrow confines either of an Oxford college, or a specific parish, and his refusal to "stay put" gave rise to endless criticism.

It was during a visit to Bristol that Wesley realised that if he was to reach the unconverted, he must preach outside the churches as well as inside them. Indeed, he claimed that it was because he was excluded from the churches, such as his father's church at Epworth, that "it remained only to preach in the open air." He did it at first, "not out of choice, but out of necessity."[32]

George Whitefield had set the example by preaching outdoors to the miners at Kingswood, near Bristol. He too had been prevented from preaching in local churches but discovered that evangelistic preaching in the open fields drew huge numbers of eager hearers. Responding to Whitefield's urgent invitation to join him in Bristol, Wesley travelled from London to witness for himself this remarkable opportunity and went with Whitefield to some of the places where he had preached to the people. April 2, 1739, was to be a significant day in the history of the evangelical revival for, during that afternoon, he "submitted to be more vile, and proclaimed in the highways the glad tidings of salvation . . . to about three thousand people." It had required a personal revolution of some magnitude for, says Wesley, he was "so tenacious at every point relating to decency and order" that he "thought the saving of souls almost a sin if it had not been done in a church."[33]

It was a memorable moment in the story of evangelism in England. What began in Bristol took him on journeys throughout England, Wales, Scotland and Ireland. Itinerants were unpopular, however, and critics were vociferous in their objections to a roving ministry. Wesley knew how to answer them. He was riding through the country in obedience to God. The call to evangelise was a biblical injunction and must not be ignored. Within a few weeks of taking up "field preaching," James Hervey, Wesley's former pupil and Holy Club colleague, wrote to say that he had hoped Wesley would return to an academic post in Oxford or accept a living and settle down somewhere in the country. If, fitful and restless, he felt unable to do that, ought he not to respect parish boundaries and wait patiently for "the right invitation?"

The committed evangelist published his reply in the *Journal*. Hervey did not understand what motivated his friend. Wesley had already received the "right invitation"; it was to share the good news with everybody he could. With apostolic conviction, Wesley told Hervey that the opportunities were limitless. He drove the point home by citing the words of the greatest itinerant of the early church in 1 Corinthians 9:16-17; like the apostle Paul, Wesley believed that "a dispensation of the gospel is committed to me; and woe is me if I preach not the gospel." Missionary work was in Wesley's veins, and if a door had closed in Georgia, another was opening in England. A man of passion was not to be silenced.

From his earliest years, he had known of the ministry of pioneer evangelists. In 1711-12 his mother had been so inspired by the account of Danish missionaries that she had decided to teach her own children the truths of Scripture one by one, allocating special time to them individually on particular days of the week. Thursday evening was set aside for "Jacky," and he never forgot either the substance of her ministry or what inspired it in the first place. The Lord of the harvest admits no boundaries.

> I look upon all the world as my parish. . . . I judge it meet, right, and my bounden duty to declare unto all that are willing to hear the glad tidings of salvation.

Hervey was anxious because Wesley's itinerancy was encouraging widespread criticism, but the preacher was not remotely troubled about that. Far from restricting his mission, it authenticated it. Some vilification is inevitable if one is to be a slave of Christ. Did Hervey not remember that from their Holy Club days?

If you ask . . . How can one do good, of whom *men say all man-ner of evil?* I will put you in mind (though you once knew this, yea, and much established me in that great truth) the more evil men say of me, for my Lord's sake, the more will he do by me. . . . How else could you ever think of "saving yourself and them that hear you" without being "the filth and off-scouring of the world"?[34]

It was difficult for Hervey and other critics to answer Wesley's logical defence of "field preaching." The *Journal*'s entries reveal why Wesley grasped every available opportunity to engage in this vigorous but costly ministry.

First, Scripture commanded it; the apostolic commission had not been withdrawn. Secondly, Christ exemplified it. The Sermon on the Mount was "one pretty remarkable precedent of field-preaching."[35] What Jesus did with such compelling effectiveness could at least be attempted by those who loved him. Thirdly, people needed it; a vast number of the millions who heard him had drifted away from the churches. Fourthly, others share it; it was not the solitary exercise some might imagine. The gathering of a huge crowd often had a humble beginning, as on one April morning at Wigton in Scotland:

The congregation, when I began, consisted of one woman, two boys, and three or four little girls, but in a quarter of an hour we had most of the town.[36]

Fifthly, the devil dislikes it. When Christ is uplifted by such passionate preaching, the enemy's strongholds are being invaded. Souls are turning from darkness to light: "Oh what a victory would Satan gain if he could put an end to field-preaching! But that I trust he never will; at least not till my head is laid."[37]

Sixthly, God uses it. Time and again, men and women were brought to personal faith as they listened to his direct and persua-sive message. People from a wide variety of different social back-grounds were dramatically transformed.

Although he continued to grasp such opportunities throughout his ministry, it must not be imagined that he ever found it easy. When he had been preaching in the open air for over thirty years, he confessed, "To this day field-preaching is a cross to me. But I know my commission and see no other way of 'preaching the gospel to every creature.'"[38]

Thousands of men and women were indebted to this persuasive and compassionate preacher. People did not always respond, but, whatever the results, he was not easily deterred. Wesley was an extrovert, even-tempered and resilient, and often attempted things he did not feel like doing. He rose at four every morning to pray, and did so whether he felt like it or not. His horse was waiting to be untied, and the journey lay before him. However he felt, he would cover the miles. Preaching was not always easy, and the news of the societies often gave rise to anxious thoughts, but he pressed on. In his wisdom he realised that there is more to life than feelings; souls without Christ might slip into a lost eternity while a man was deciding whether he felt like preaching to them or not.

Tireless in his devotion to others, Wesley was rarely still and unoccupied. Widely travelled and well-read, he would have been an ideal companion for a long, relaxed talk, but he rarely indulged in such luxuries. Samuel Johnson was irritated by his preoccupation with the next task.

> John Wesley's conversation is good, but he is never at leisure. He is obliged to go at a certain hour. This is very disagreeable to a man who loves to fold his legs and have out his talk, as I do.[39]

Wesley preferred to walk his legs rather than fold them.

Yet, it is a mistake to relegate his vigorous evangelism to a bygone chapter in English church history. His zeal to reach people who did not know Christ has something to say to late twentieth-century believers about the importance of personal witness. At great personal cost he grasped an opportunity for outdoor preaching and recognised that, for him, it was the best way of reaching the maximum number of people in eighteenth-century Britain. As we read a great spiritual classic like his *Journal*, we need to ask ourselves in what way we might best reach our contemporaries.

Like him, we are commanded by Scripture to do so, and Christ is our great exemplar. Jesus was as concerned to talk with individuals as to address crowds. As in Wesley's day, men and women from every possible social background urgently need the message of Christ's persistent love, unique sacrifice and promised pardon. As Wesley proved, if we venture to share the good news with others, we need not do so as isolated individuals. Others will become our partners by their example, prayers, experience, skills and support. We too will discover with Wesley that the devil will not like it. A silent Christian is no threat to him, but one who is prepared to speak about Christ is a powerful instrument in the hands of God. Wesley's experience was that however fierce the opposition, when Christ was lovingly proclaimed, people were won. The love of Christ was the heart of their message, and love for Christ was the secret of their strength.

Love for the Believers—the Importance of Fellowship

It was part of the genius of Wesley's ministry that his converts were immediately introduced into local well-organised cells for teaching and fellowship. Wherever in the country his extensive influence had reached, there was one of his societies. In commencing the work of the societies, it was never Wesley's intention to draw Christians away from the parish churches or any other congregation. They were to supplement the work of the churches, not replace them. The formation of societies was born out of a natural desire to see new converts going on in the life of holiness. Good seed, however well sown, would not grow in the poor soil of an unhelpful church. He told Mary Bishop, a fellow worker in Bath, that "the great work" was not only to bring souls to personal faith, but to build them up in their faith.

"How grievously are they mistaken . . . who imagine that as

soon as the children are born, they need take no more care of them! We do not find it so. The chief care then begins."[40]

His first society was formed in London and met at a place known as the Foundery, near Moorfields. Prior to that, Wesley and his London friends had met with a Moravian congregation in Fetter Lane, but an unhelpful aspect of their teaching at that time caused Wesley and others to withdraw and begin their own society. The Foundery was a derelict building, earlier used for casting cannon, and although obtained for a reasonable price, the London Methodists spent a considerable sum to make it suitable for their purposes. Living accommodation was provided as a London base for Wesley, and the Foundery soon came to be regarded as head-quarters for the work in England.

The life and work of the societies was governed by a set of rules drawn up by their founder. The single condition for joining was a desire for personal salvation. Members were expected to give prac-tical expression to this desire by a commitment to attend public worship, engage in frequent prayer (both personally and in fami-lies), practise fasting, read the Bible, avoid inconsistent behaviour and use every opportunity to do good. As Wesley toured the coun-try, he frequently reminded the Methodist people of their obliga-tions and responsibilities as society members, sometimes using his visit to explain the rules, their value and purpose.

Each society was divided into smaller classes, an idea that may owe something to childhood recollections of life at Epworth. During a period when her husband was away at Convocation, Susannah Wesley commenced a Sunday evening meeting in the rectory kitchen originally intended for her children and servants, but when news of the event got around, others asked if they might come, and numbers continued to grow until the spacious room was packed to capacity. At this time John was a highly impressionable nine-year-old, and the clear memory of these occasions for teach-ing, prayer and encouragement remained throughout his life. When his mother died, his *Journal* account of the funeral included her earlier description and defence of these kitchen meetings.[41]

The organisation of the Methodist class was basic and uncomplicated. Each had an appointed leader responsible for the general supervision and pastoral care of the group, and, if taken seriously, the duties were demanding. Leaders were expected to make weekly contact with their members and, if appropriate, use the occasion to enquire lovingly about their spiritual welfare. The leader was also expected to collect from every member a weekly contribution for people in financial need.

Further smaller groups known as bands were also guided by rules. They met each week to share their recent spiritual experience and realistically admit their failures as they sought the prayer support of their fellow members.

The opportunities taken by the society for meeting were not to coincide with normal Sunday worship hours. Toward the end of his life, Wesley told a colleague, "I advise all our brethren that have been brought up in the Church to continue there. . . . The Methodists are to spread life among all denominations."[42] Wesley hoped that the vigorous life of the societies would encourage a deeper devotion in the local churches, but the dream was not always fulfilled.

In the course of his journeys, Wesley found increasing delight in the work of the societies and was pleased with every opportunity to enrich their life and expand their witness. He was pleased to use the *Journal* as a vehicle for relevant Christian education. Each entry served to make the Methodists more aware of what God was doing in other places. If they encountered fierce opposition, they heard how their fellow believers were helped in harassing circumstances, while other entries showed that some local communities, once noted for bitter persecution, had been astonishingly transformed. For all his high standards and demanding ethical principles, Wesley was a great encourager. Critics might accuse him of autocracy, but everything was motivated by love.

There were occasions when genuine love was expressed in constructive, at times painful, criticism. An example of Wesley's artistry in handling people is demonstrated in his consistent openness and honesty with the societies. This is particularly reflected in the way he refused to indulge in flattery when he visited them or silently to overlook obvious faults. In the interests of harmony and unity, some men might have turned a blind eye to inconsistencies, but Wesley knew that his people were likely to take a rebuke from him that they might find hurtful from a local leader. If something was wrong, he grasped the opportunity to tell them plainly while he could.

During a visit to East Anglia, he preached at Lakenheath to "an honest, drowsy people," and, though that cannot have been very cheering, when he reached Norwich, he found himself expounding Scripture to "a large, rude, noisy congregation." He had little intention of tolerating irreverent behaviour; he was "determined to mend them or end them" and told them frankly how to behave at worship.[43]

Just over a week later, he preached at a village only a few miles from Norwich. The believers who turned up for their 7 A.M. meeting must have had an early morning shock when he "told them in plain terms that they were the most ignorant, self-conceited, self-willed, fickle, untractable, disorderly, disjointed society" that he knew. But it says something for their resilience that when "God applied it to their hearts . . . many were profited," and he did "not find one that was offended."[44]

Wesley's critics frequently castigated him as a dictatorial autocrat, and there is little doubt that he forcefully insisted on good conduct in the society. We must remember that during the revival, large numbers of people who were not accustomed to worship were drawn into the ranks of the Methodists. When he visited their meetings, there was frequent need for objective assessment and honest correction, as well as forthright biblical exposition.

A keen observer of human behaviour, Wesley knew how easily human relationships could be damaged. The societies must be warned about the perils of an uncontrolled tongue. Gossip is always perilous, so he made it a principle never to accept anything on hearsay. The Christian world of his day was scarcely ever free from altercations of one kind or another. Disputes and controversies were a constant drain on thought and time. Somewhere in the country, somebody or other was busily writing a pamphlet attacking someone else. In such fractious contexts it was easy to build up a mistaken perception of an opponent merely because someone had said or written something about his unorthodox teaching or scandalous conduct.

Wesley's own message was exposed to widespread criticism; antagonists of all theological shades and ecclesiastical sympathies constantly challenged his theology. They maintained that his doctrine of salvation for all was unbiblical, his message of assurance presumptuous, and his idea of holiness absurd. With so many critics, he made it his business never to accept a statement as truth merely because someone had said it of his opponent's polemic or claimed to have read it in one of their writings. He had to hear or read it for himself; until then, however pressed for an opinion, he would suspend judgment on the matter.

In the year following his return from Georgia, he had occasion to prove how mistaken someone can be. After what happened in Aldersgate Street, he wrote a short account of his experience that night and over the succeeding weeks. He read it to his mother, who "greatly approved it, and said she heartily blessed God" for bringing her son "to so just a way of thinking." Soon after, he left England to visit Moravian friends in Germany, and while he was away, a copy of that written account was sent without his knowledge to his unsympathetic brother Samuel. He, in turn, related the details verbally to his mother. Susannah Wesley was deeply disturbed by what she heard from Samuel. Wesley says he found his mother "under strange fears concerning me, being convinced 'by an account taken from one of my own papers that I had greatly erred from the faith.'"

Wesley was astonished by his mother's distress; he "could not conceive what the paper could be," but on careful enquiry he discovered that "it was the same paper I had read her myself." He had learned a lesson he was never to forget:

> How hard is it to form a true judgment of any person or thing from the account of a prejudiced relater! Yea, though he be

ever so honest a man—for he who gave this relation was one of unquestionable veracity. And yet by his *sincere* account of a writing which lay before his eyes was the truth so totally disguised that my mother knew not the paper she had heard from end to end, nor I that I had myself wrote.[45]

Wesley also knew how to deal effectively with cranks. In the course of his travels, he was bound to meet more than his fair share of eccentrics. One example illustrates his ability in handling trouble from an unexpected source. Church leaders and others have occasionally been embarrassed by men or women who claim to have received special revelations of God's will for someone else; such practice can become manipulative, even destructive, in relationships. He gave one London sister short shrift. She came to him "as she said, with a message from the Lord." It was "to tell me I was laying up treasures on earth, taking my ease, and minding only my eating and drinking. I told her, God knew me better; and, if He had sent her, He would have sent her with a more proper message."[46]

Publishing such encounters in the *Journal* must have gone some way to warn genuine believers that one can be mistaken in private revelations, and may have protected Wesley from similar excesses over the years that followed. To denounce him, of all people, of materialism, laziness and gluttony was a cruel accusation and a reminder that sincere people can be totally misled when they profess to receive guidance for others.

He was always outspoken on ethical issues. Societies were not likely to make an effective impact on the local community if neighbours could accuse them of improper conduct or moral indiscretions. Smuggling disturbed him greatly, especially when he visited coastal areas. In Cornwall he began examining one society, but "was soon obliged to stop short" when he found that "well nigh one and all bought or sold uncustomed goods." He told them plainly that "they must put this abomination away, or they would see my face no more."[47]

Publicising his disapproval of such practices and warning that he would not visit offending societies naturally affected readers who wavered on such issues. If numbers were low in a society, local leaders might be tempted to overlook smuggling, but in the pages of the *Journal* the Methodist leader made it clear that stealing can never be right. Smugglers were robbing their country. By putting the matter right, the Sunderland believers had increased their numbers; but even if they had not, Wesley was firmly convinced that it was better to honour God's word than worship statistics.

> Most of the robbers, commonly called smugglers, have left us; but more than twice their number of honest people are already come in their place. And if none had come, yet should I not dare to keep those who steal either from the King or subject.[48]

As he travelled the country, Wesley noticed that "since that accursed thing has been put away, the work of God has everywhere increased." At Port Isaac in the West country the society had "more than doubled; and they are all alive to God."[49]

His repeated use in this context of the phrase "the accursed thing" deliberately recalled the Achan story in Joshua 7; smuggling was theft, and wherever practised, it would mar the spiritual effectiveness of the local Christians.

Wesley used his ministry among the societies to encourage, inspire, teach, stimulate, challenge, warn, advise and correct his fellow believers. We all have a responsibility to help other Christians. The Bible knows nothing about a "do-it-yourself" believer. In New Testament imagery, we are limbs in the same body, stones in the one temple. We are expected to contribute to one another's life in Christ. I have heard it described as "one-anothering." It is said that the Bible has about twenty-four references to "one another"; we are to love, support, serve, encourage one another, to name but a few. As with most of their great themes, Charles Wesley helped the Methodist people to learn this truth through the verses of a hymn:

He bids us build each other up,
And gathered into one
To our high calling's glorious hope
We hand in hand go on.

Reflecting on the work of Wesley and his partners in the societies might stir us to put some crucial questions to ourselves: Does the contribution I make in my church build other Christians up? How genuine, impartial, practical and sacrificial is my love for other believers? Does the quality of my personal lifestyle enhance the corporate testimony of the church in our local community?

Love for the Unloved—the Privilege of Caring

Love has no boundaries. It cannot be narrowly confined within the walls of a church. The radical holiness teaching of John's First Epistle was always important for Wesley. He loved its message of freedom from sin and its equal insistence that believers must not love in word only, but in deed and truth. Moreover, such love must be uninhibited in extent and practical in expression. "Perfect love" was evident in his passionate social concern.

Early in his London ministry, he provided winter employment for deprived men who were on the threshold of destitution. To their newly acquired premises, they welcomed "the poorest, and a teacher, into the society-room, where they were employed for four months, till spring came on, in carding and spinning of cotton."[50]

Wherever he travelled, he was always concerned for the hungry and homeless. He had experienced poverty in childhood and could never ignore the needs of deprived people. On visiting Bristol in 1759, he was shocked when he saw over a thousand French prisoners of war at Knowle suffering extreme hardship during a severe winter. They were "without anything to lie on but a little dirty straw, or anything to cover them but a few foul, thin rags, either by day or night, so that they died like rotten sheep. I was much affected."

Wesley knew where to find the best text for any occasion. That night he preached a sermon on Exodus 23:9: "Thou shalt not oppress a stranger; for ye know the heart of a stranger, seeing ye were strangers in the land of Egypt." His congregation was immediately responsive. An offering was taken at the service, quickly supplemented by further gifts the following day. Jesus had anticipated such a moment: "I needed clothes and you clothed me." So with the money they had raised, they "bought linen and woollen cloth, which were made up into shirts, waistcoats, and breeches. Some dozens of stockings were added," and all "were carefully distributed where there was the greatest want."

Wesley did more. He could use his pen for the prisoners as well as his voice. He wrote a moving description of their needs, and his appeal was published in *Lloyd's Evening Post*, resulting in increased gifts from London and other parts of the country.[51]

This practical compassion continued throughout his life. His last letter was written a week before he died, to encourage Wilberforce in his campaign against the slave trade, "that execrable villainy." For years he had refused sugar because it was bought at the price of cruelty. Wilberforce and his colleagues were encountering considerable opposition, and so, anxious that the great campaigner should not be "worn out by the opposition of men and devils," Wesley urged him to press on, "in the name of God, and in the power of His might, till even American slavery (the vilest that ever saw the sun) shall vanish away before it."[52]

Wesley's concern for people took precedence over all else. Clothes were regularly distributed to the poor,[53] and he was always troubled about those unemployed "without their own fault." Visiting the destitute in London during the winter of 1753, he reflected that they were worse off than poverty-stricken Indians he had met, for in Georgia their own people would help them, whereas in London, hundreds died unrelieved and unnoticed:

> I found some in their cells under ground, others in their garrets, half starved both with cold and hunger, added to weak-

ness and pain. So wickedly, devilishly false is that common objection, "They are poor only because they are idle." If you saw these things with your own eyes, could you lay out money in ornaments or superfluities?[54]

Among huge numbers of hungry people in the metropolis, "many are sick and ready to perish." He had done everything possible to help but could not meet such immense needs on his own. Always practical, Wesley urged his members to share with him in this ministry by bringing whatever clothes they could spare and by donating a penny a week, "or what they could afford," to help others.

He again initiated a scheme whereby knitting provided employment, this time for a number of women, and appointed a team of twelve to make arrangements for the practical care of needy people. In order to ensure that the essential relief work was carried out efficiently, he asked that the workers meet together "to give an account of what they have done, and consult what can be done farther."[55] The example of what was happening at the Foundery encouraged similar initiatives elsewhere.

The popular impression of Wesley is of the tireless itinerant evangelist, but it is important to remember the wide range of his social concern. We have noticed his work for prisoners of war, slaves, the poor, hungry, sick and unemployed, but in addition he made practical arrangements for the care of orphans, encouraged the regular visitation of men and women in prisons, and opened schools.

Ours is an entirely different society, and in so many ways we should be grateful for that. Many areas of social deprivation with which Wesley and his colleagues were actively concerned are now managed by the State, but believers who love their neighbour will be sensitive to vast needs that can never be met by government agencies alone. Our world is teeming with millions who are poor, hungry, destitute and homeless, and in this global village they are our neighbours whose needs are as near as our television screens.

The latest Tear Fund figures tell us that 1,000 million of our neighbours will go to bed hungry tonight; people whose hearts are filled with Christ's love cannot possibly be unconcerned. Spirituality means sacrifice for us as much as for Wesley's partners. That may mean missing a meal once in each week in order to donate the money we would have spent on food to help supply the needs of those who would rejoice to have one really good meal a week. Do those searching words not haunt us: "I was hungry and you did not feed me"?

For some it may mean giving time, a more precious commodity than money in many lives. Perhaps there is some person in need, dispirited, perplexed, unwell or lonely, and we ought to call on him or her, anticipating what Christ might say: "I was sick and you visited me."

It is said that when Mother Teresa visited a home for elderly people in the USA, she asked two questions on leaving. Why were the residents unsmiling, and, as they sat together in that large room, why were they all facing the door? The answer to both questions was brief and penetrating: "They are waiting for someone to come." Are you that "someone" in the life of a friend, acquaintance, neighbour or fellow church member? Kindness is love in action. There is no spirituality without love, and in New Testament terms love is suspect if it does not issue in practical help.

Wesley loved people, but he knew that Christian work can never be effectively motivated by mere altruism. Something more is necessary than an awareness of human need. The motivation and compulsion to serve, whether by evangelistic witness, pastoral care or practical help, must be Christ's love within us. If we rely on our own resources, the limited strength is likely to fail. But those who love Christ more than they love themselves, or even more than they love others, will be freshly energised for each opportunity. The power to persist will never be lacking.

And What About Us?

Our four writers exercised an influence on Christian thought far beyond their native countries, and their ministry as spiritual leaders has extended throughout history, reaching our own times. We shall now look back over their special books to summarise what these men might be saying to us about spirituality today. Ten themes are of continuing relevance in the contemporary world. They urge us to:

OFFER OUR WORSHIP

These four Christians recognised the priority of praise. Augustine's testimony is a sacrifice of adoring thanksgiving acknowledging that a God of mercy lovingly pursued an arrogant rebel. Luther advises his barber friend to meditate daily on the Ten Commandments, the Lord's Prayer and the Creed to ensure that each day fresh material in his "hymn book" recalls his debt and inspires his worship. Bunyan is stunned with gratitude as he surveys his story, his great transgressions obliterated by a great God:

> O the remembrance of my great sins, of my great temptations, and of my great fears of perishing forever! They bring fresh into my mind the remembrance of my great help, my great support from heaven, and the great grace that God extended to such a wretch as I.[1]

As soon as the Wesley brothers were converted, they voiced their gratitude in a rhapsody of praise. After leaving that Aldersgate Street room in the late evening, John was "brought in triumph" by a group of friends to the home where Charles was staying. As they burst in, John called out, "I believe," and "with great joy" they sang a hymn Charles had written to mark his own conversion a few days earlier. It captured these essential notes of adoration and thanksgiving:

> *Where shall my wondering soul begin?*
> *How shall I all to heaven aspire?*
> *A slave redeemed from death and sin,*
> *A brand plucked from eternal fire,*
> *How shall I equal triumphs raise,*
> *Or sing my great Deliverer's praise?*
>
> *O how shall I the goodness tell,*
> *Father, which Thou to me hast showed?*
> *That I, a child of wrath and hell,*
> *I should be called a child of God,*
> *Should know, should feel my sins forgiven,*
> *Blest with this antepast of heaven!*

That adoring wonder continued through to Wesley's final hours, as his weak voice took up the words of Isaac Watts:

> *I'll praise my Maker while I've breath;*
> *And when my voice is lost in death,*
> *Praise shall employ my nobler powers . . .*

Adoration is the authentic mark of genuine spirituality, whatever the century. Let Augustine be our example. He glorifies God throughout the *Confessions*, praising him for natural endowments ("gifts of my God: I did not give them to myself"), for the miracle of forgiveness, for his personal love ("caring for each one of us as though the only one in your care, and yet for all as for each individual") and for his providential direction through a labyrinth of frustrating experiences. He magnifies God for his correction, his patience in following him over heedless years of spiritual ignorance and moral rebellion, even for creating such restless discontent:

> Glory to you, fount of mercies. As I became unhappier, you drew closer. Your right hand was by me, already prepared to snatch me out of the filth, and to clean me up. But I did not know it.[2]

Augustine is an inspiring example of the supremely grateful saint. Released from a preoccupation with themselves, those who walk the way of holiness have a passion for God. They are devoted to others; yet they have not escaped the tyranny of self-interest by diverting their attention to other people, but by gazing upon God. Their love for him is renewed in regular devotion, and they are not content unless Scripture, the testimony of others, or their own experience in each day yields some fresh discovery of the nature and sufficiency of God.

RECORD OUR EXPERIENCE

Moreover, these discoveries are best preserved in writing, or the gratitude quickly evaporates. Writing demands concentration of mind, clarifies our convictions, records our debts and impresses truth upon the memory. The written word is an abiding testimony to a grateful past. Putting things down on paper is an important yet neglected aspect of the devotional life.

Augustine, Luther, Bunyan and Wesley were committed writers. Much as they valued their opportunities for preaching, each took the trouble to preserve his experience in written form. Augustine exalts God's patience with a prejudiced runaway. Luther tells a friend how he is daily welcomed into a Father's presence, the dependent child sure to be heard. Bunyan rejoices that God's mercy is inexhaustible, and Wesley affirms God's compassion for a loveless world. Each of their four books is in the nature of personal written testimony. Meditations and reflections such as these are easily lost. They are best set down in writing as Christians of earlier days were eager to do.

The English Puritans encouraged the keeping of journals and provide numerous examples of this rewarding spiritual discipline. In his book *The Journal or Diary of a Thankful Christian* (1656), John Beadle argues that tradesmen, merchants, lawyers, physicians and house-holders should all keep written records of their work, and Christians, accountable to God, can gain spiritually by keeping a daily journal. Edmund Staunton kept a "diary of God's mercies." John Carter had a book "in which every day he set down . . . whatsoever memorable things he had heard or read that day."[3] Later, Wesley commended diary-keeping to his preachers, helping them to see that it was a use-ful way of expressing their accountability to God and enriching the spiritual life. Wherever he travelled, he commended the practice of writing personal accounts of Christian experience, and his people were often pleased to take his advice, leaving a store of enriching devotional literature, much of which appeared in print.[4]

Many contemporary Christians are rediscovering the value of keeping a journal to record their fresh spiritual discoveries.[5] Those who keep diaries of this kind set aside some time every day for quiet reflection on the activity of God. Three things are prominent in their meditation.

First, they search their Bibles, contemplating who God is. To every scriptural passage they pose their urgent question: What do these verses convey to me about the majesty of God, the uniqueness of Christ, the ministry of the Spirit? They then set down their find-ings in writing. Each day yields some new insight or fresh reminder of God in his triune greatness.

Second, in examining their experience, Christians recall what God does. He is not separated from them by a remote distance, but is intimately involved in their lives. Reflecting on each day, believ-ers think carefully about how God has acted for them—warning, protecting, strengthening, guiding, encouraging, rebuking, forgiv-ing and using them. There are important lessons to be learned from these daily experiences, and they are best recorded in writing. Recollection prompts adoration.

Augustine came to see that God was at work in his life even when he was not aware of divine intervention. The Lord was touching him emotionally through the death of a friend, intellectually through frustration over religion, vocationally through painful disappointment about students, morally through his unsatisfying lifestyle and spiritually through the prayers of his mother, the preaching of Ambrose and the testimony of other Christians. Luther's pre-conversion uncertainties, Bunyan's long imprisonment and Wesley's failures in Georgia were all used in the sovereignty of God, and these men considered their experiences worth recording.

Third, in looking out on society, Christians also discern where God is manifesting himself in the modern world even when people do not recognise him. God's interests have never been confined solely to religion. He is sovereignly at work in the twentieth century as much as he was in the time of the Old Testament prophets who saw beyond the geographical boundaries of Israel and Judah to the great empires of their time. Assyria was the rod of God's anger, a Babylonian king his servant, and a Persian prince his shepherd (Is 10:5; Jer 43:10; Is 44:28).

Augustine witnessed the disintegration of the Roman Empire, but it prompted him to write one of his greatest books. The barbarian hordes were besieging Hippo during his final hours, but he knew that God's kingdom would outlive both Romans and Vandals and every other dominating power in the world. He had big maps. Centuries later he inspired Luther to sing:

> *These things shall vanish all,*
> *The city of God remaineth.*

When Luther wrote his book for Peter Beskendorf, he encouraged him to pray for the godless world, for people holding responsible positions in local and national leadership and for those who hate the church as well as for all who love it. Wesley's horizons were not limited to the Methodist people; he interested himself in national affairs, preached about issues of contemporary concern and prayed intelligently about them too. His first book, a collection of prayers "for every day in the week," reveals not only his concern for discipline in prayer but also the breadth of his vision and the all-inclusive nature of his daily intercessions. He did not believe in a narrowly blinkered prayer life but one that embraced the needs of community, nation and world.[6] He was as passionate about humiliated slaves in America as about the disadvantaged poor in England. Modern Christians must not live in isolation from the world but in full awareness of God's sovereign involvement in the affairs of communities and nations as well as individuals. Issues of this kind find a place in their prayers and in their journals.

UTILISE OUR TIME

All four of these men were well-organised people. The fact that, in different contexts, they contributed so extensively to the life and thought of the Christian community was due largely to their personal discipline. The idle will never achieve. Augustine worked energetically—preaching, counselling, studying, writing—year after year in that North African seaport, and his message reached the world. Luther produced almost a book a fortnight, from short tracts on pastoral issues to works of great substance. Between his writing assignments, he was lecturing on the Bible, preaching regularly to an expectant congregation, translating Scripture into the German language, helping people personally by conversations and letters, compiling a hymn book and being as good a husband and father as he knew how to be.

For a huge section of his adult life, Bunyan was denied the freedom to be the husband and father he wanted to be, but he too redeemed the time by studying the Bible, thinking about God, writing books, talking about life and eternity with his fellow prisoners and preaching whenever and wherever he could. Wesley's days always moved through a succession of well-planned events, ordered by a fine sense of balance between necessary structure and compassionate flexibility. Influenced by a Puritan background and by seventeenth-century writers, he planned each day "according to rule," and therein lies the secret of his success.

Our days will be different from theirs, but we too must regard time as God's priceless gift, as easily squandered and misused as all his other benefits. We can hardly compete with the enormous output of these men, but that need not deter us from setting prayerfully determined goals in our own lives or from adopting the disciplined lifestyle that made their attainment possible.

We must buy up the spare minutes and not waste our emotional energy longing for expansive stretches with leisurely hours in which we can read and pray. Francois Fenelon, the French spiritual writer, used to say that we must "make good use of chance moments," as when we are waiting for someone or travelling:

> At such times it is easy to lift the heart to God, and thereby gain fresh strength for further duties. One moment will suffice to place yourself in God's presence, to love and worship Him. If you wait for free, convenient seasons in which to fulfil real duties, you run the risk of waiting forever.

Fenelon insists: "The less time one has, the more carefully it should be husbanded."[7] Spirituality has a lot to do with the creative handling of time. If that is absent, prayer is likely to be a precarious and spasmodic exercise and spiritual progress a distant dream.

PLAN OUR PRAYING

Our four guides were men of prayer. Luther has provided us with a detailed account of how he prayed. We can summarise seven of its lessons. His *Simple Way* helped his barber to pray *dependently*, knowing that there are hidden foes and dangers, far more in the vulnerable, unguarded areas of his own life than Peter Beskendorf could have imagined. We are frail creatures without God's strength, and men or women who do not pray face the hazards of life unaided. Prayerlessness is practical atheism. Failure to pray is a silent witness to our arrogant independence and insular self-confidence. It is one way of telling God that we are perfectly capable of looking after ourselves.

Luther's book illustrates how to pray *imaginatively*, allowing the biblical material to provide four "books" of helpful meditation. The Reformer wants his friend to pray *confidently*, so that by his firm concluding "amen," he may be assured that his prayer has certainly been heard. It is also important to pray *relevantly*, touching on some of the great issues of our time, compassionately bringing the needs of the world into the presence of a caring God.

Luther hopes Peter Beskendorf will pray *appreciatively*, supremely grateful for God's creative power (making something new even of his bleak life in exile), for Christ's saving work (covering his transgressions) and for the Spirit's empowering ministry by which alone he can be sustained. Luther hopes he will also be thankful for the redeemed people of God to whom he belongs, knowing that whenever he prays in distant Dessau, separated from all he knows best and loves most, his fellow believers back in Wittenberg, and praying Christians throughout the world, are standing alongside him in faith, hope and love. Peter the barber is urged to pray *attentively*, not devoting the time to constant begging. By reverent and submissive listening, he opens his mind to what God wants to say to him, bringing the spirit of joyful obedience to whatever the Lord requires.

Prayer must be planned, or it may become haphazard, diffuse or repetitively boring. Such planning will not be easy; the devil subtly lures us away to other things. Bunyan's testimony highlights the need to pray *persistently*, resisting the devil's distractions when he urges us to "have done, break off, make haste, you have prayed enough, and stay no longer. . . . "

We shall always need to pray because the enemy is ruthlessly determined to cool our spiritual passion; he tried hard with Bunyan:

I will cool you insensibly, by degrees, by little and little; what care I, saith he, though I be seven years in chilling your heart, if I can do it at last; continual rocking will lull a crying child asleep. I will ply it close, but I will have my end accomplished: though you be burning hot at present, yet, if I can pull you from this fire, I shall have you cold before it be long.[8]

Prayer will be costly, and we may have to pay the price in sleep (like Wesley, rising earlier than usual) or in pleasure, occasionally sacrificing some alternative activity in order to devote more time to God. Unless we plan it, we will not do it. In the end, it has little to do with inclination but everything to do with organisation. If we want something in life badly enough, we will sacrifice anything to obtain it. People with spiritual priorities long only for God, and prayer is their lifeline.

KNOW OUR BIBLES

Our four leaders were great lovers of Scripture, though with at least two of them it had not always been so. Augustine had little time for it when a copy first came into his hands, and though Bunyan possessed a Bible, he did not come to terms with its message until those Bedford women shared "with what words and promises they had been refreshed." They spoke not only with joy, but "with such pleasantness of Scripture language" that he too longed for the "new world" they had found in Christ. Their testimony drove him to Scripture, and in time, he became one of its more imaginative interpreters. Luther and Wesley had known the Bible from their earliest years, though with both of them it was necessary to receive what Bunyan's pastor, John Gifford, called "evidence from heaven" before they could claim personal faith in Christ.

The Bible was vital for all four, and their writings urge us to find a place in every day to read it systematically (following some methodical plan of study) and meditatively, recalling Luther's "four books" once again. It must be read expectantly, believing that

God will speak to us through its pages as clearly as he addressed Augustine in a Milan garden, Luther as he pored over Romans in his Wittenberg study, Bunyan in the Bedfordshire countryside and Wesley in that London meeting room. To some, the transforming word came dramatically, sharply focusing its message at a precise moment of time. For others, like Bunyan, the impact, though memorable, was more gradual. Augustine, Luther and Wesley knew in a moment. With Bunyan, it was a couple of years before the peace came; but, throughout his long search, the word worked on.

No Christian can develop an informed and resourceful spirituality without Scripture. If we would grow in the knowledge of God, we must hear what he says, and that demands a set time every day.

ORGANISE OUR READING

Although these men owed a unique debt to Scripture, they also discovered new dimensions of grace through the writings of other believers. Augustine was helped by hearing about Antony, whose life had been written by Athanasius in the fourth century. Antony first discerned the call of Christ through listening to the biblical narrative concerning the rich young ruler, but unlike the ruler, he determined to follow immediately. Augustine made Antony's response his own. The written account of Antony's abandonment to Christ was instrumental in prompting Augustine's own desire for commitment.

Luther was also indebted to great Christian writing; references to Augustine crowd his pages. Bunyan was grateful for Luther; when that tattered copy of his *Commentary on Galatians* fell into the tinker's hands, it became a book treasured above all others, apart from the Bible. That same commentary was used to convince Charles Wesley and led directly to his Whit Sunday conversion. The following Wednesday his brother heard a reading from Luther, and that evening the certainty came. These men were indebted to Scripture and were helped enormously by its inspired interpreters.

Reading continued to be important throughout their lives.

Augustine was always pleased to receive a good book. Luther drew widely on the writings of others. As a prisoner, Bunyan had little access to books, but in his cell he treasured Foxe's *Book of Martyrs* and Vavasor Powell's helpful *Concordance*; and in earlier days, alongside his Luther, there were those two Puritan books that set his heart on pilgrimage.

Wesley was a keen reader, and in the *Journal* he frequently mentioned the latest book, telling others what he made of it. He knew that good reading widens the believer's horizons. His famous *Christian Library* was initiated to make popular editions and abridgements available at reasonable cost. Its fifty volumes included the apostolic fathers from the early church period, several of the great Puritan writings (admiring "their perpetual quest for Christ") and those seventeenth-century authors who had influenced him deeply, such as Jeremy Taylor and George Herbert. There were continental writers on the spiritual life—for example, Pascal, Fenelon and Madame Guyon—and biographies of great Reformers such as Luther, Calvin and Peter Martyr. Scottish authors had their place: Henry Scougal, Robert Leighton and Samuel Rutherford. All these testify to Wesley's wide sympathies and his indebtedness to people far beyond the Church of England. The *Christian Library* was not a financial success and may not have been used as widely as he hoped, but Methodists who read such books drew from a well of deep devotion.

Christian reading promotes spiritual development. It feeds our minds, concentrates our thoughts on great biblical themes and enables us to enter into the experience of other believers. In realising the immensity of their problems, we discover fresh resources to face our own. Reading enlarges our vision of God and provides us with new perspectives on Christian witness, holiness and service.

If we are to benefit from reading, that too needs to be planned, so that our selection of books is balanced and our time profitably spent. Many outstanding Christian classics wait to be explored. Bernard of Clairvaux on the love of God is a treasure of meditative devotion. Wesley found a place in his *Christian Library* for the

Imitation of Christ by Thomas à Kempis, a book that brought John Newton to acknowledge his need of Christ. William Law's *Serious Call to a Devout and Holy Life* played a crucial role in Wesley's pre-conversion experience.

Spiritually enriching books do not belong solely to the past. In our own time, James Packer's *Knowing God* has inspired thousands of Christians who have used it devotionally since it was first published twenty years ago. More recently, John Stott's *Cross of Christ* has reminded believers throughout the world of the nature, effects and contemporary relevance of what was achieved by God's Son on that first Good Friday. James M. Gordon's *Evangelical Spirituality* is a heart-warming exposition of the theme, covering the period from the Wesleys to the present day.

Apart from the spiritual inspiration provided by its content, good Christian reading helps us to realise our immense debt to the whole people of God. Quality Christian literature reminds us that the saints are everywhere, which leads us to our next theme.

PRIZE OUR PARTNERS

All four of our writers were deeply indebted to others and could not have accomplished a fraction of what they did without the inspiration, love and practical support of fellow Christians. Augustine was pursued by the prayers of his believing mother, taught by the gifted preaching of Ambrose, encouraged by the pastoral care of Simplicianus (the man who passed on the courageous testimony of the elderly Victorinus) and uplifted by the conversation of Ponticianus, the first to tell him the story of Antony's conversion. Each of these people played some part in bringing Augustine to convinced personal faith.

Throughout life, Luther valued his colleagues and Christian friends; and Bunyan was ever indebted to those Bedford women who sat in a doorway in the sun, talking winsomely of Christ, as well as to the preaching of John Gifford and the attractive example of his congregation. John Wesley reminded the early Methodist people that "the Bible knows nothing of solitary religion."

Spirituality does not develop in isolation from other believers. Christians need to ensure that their spiritual life relates closely to that of others. When Jesus wanted to establish his work on earth, he gathered disciples around him. The number of twelve was significant; for centuries the twelve tribes represented their nation in its unity. He taught them as a group (the name "disciple" means "learner") and encouraged them to help each other, sending them out to preach and serve in twos so that they could support one another. Jesus also derived personal help from their discipleship; at the end of his earthly life he thanked them that they had stood by him in his tribulations and testings (Lk 22:28).

All the New Testament writers underlined the importance of partnership by using metaphors and images that illustrate the interdependence of Christians. Paul said that we are like limbs in a body that needs coordinating harmony if it is to work effectively. Peter used the imagery of a building, portraying Christians as "living stones" built together in a spiritual temple, enjoying solidarity in each other's faith (1 Pet 2:5). When the gifted author of Hebrews wrote to help believers threatened by renewed persecution, he urged the same principle: "Let us not give up meeting together, as some are in the habit of doing, but let us encourage one another" (Heb 10:25). James emphasises the supportive ministry of mutual prayer (Jas 5:16); and John's First Epistle underlines the importance of practical mutual love (1 Jn 3:16-18, 23; 4:7-8, 19-21). We belong to one another in the church of Christ, and authentic spirituality is expressed within the partnership of our fellow believers—supporting, challenging, inspiring, uplifting, even correcting us when necessary.

IDENTIFY OUR GIFTS

Reading about great Christians from earlier times and living alongside our fellow believers in the contemporary world ought to stimulate us to dedicated service for Christ. Healthy Christian living depends on regular opportunities for service. All four of the people we have studied became imaginative contributors to the work of Christ's kingdom, though with different gifts.

Biblical spirituality finds a natural outlet in some form of regular, dependent, committed service to Christ. It may not always be within the walls of a church; his work has never been confined to ecclesiastical buildings. Once again we are back to this crucial issue of the allocation of time. In dependence on God, Christians discern what their precise gifts are and where they can best be used in the work of Christ.

A key passage is 1 Peter 4:10-11. The apostle knew that the work of those Christian communities scattered throughout Asia Minor could only be maintained, deepened and extended through the vigorous service of their entire membership and not simply by the dedicated work of a select minority. In these verses Peter says that believers use God's gifts in God's strength for God's glory. He shares five things here about the manner in which God allocates gifts.

He distributes them *widely*. We are all gifted people: "Each one should use whatever gift he has received." We cannot excuse ourselves as being ungifted when the apostle clearly tells us that no believer is bypassed at the distribution of God's gifts.

They are dispersed *separately*; there is a delightful individuality about the gifts of God. Nobody is gifted in precisely the same way as anybody else. Augustine could write massive doctrinal tomes, but Wesley was better at communicating the message in the open air to vast crowds. Luther was immensely gifted as a theologian, but he did not possess the literary skills to produce a brilliant story such as *Pilgrim's Progress*.

Moreover, God distributes his gifts *generously*. They are described by Peter as "grace in its various forms." The word literally means "many-coloured"; it is used in 1:6 to describe our different trials. Our adversities are not identical, nor our gifts. There is nothing monochrome about them. What one person cannot possibly attempt is gladly undertaken by someone else. One task demands alert intellectual skills, another requires immense physical energy, and another constant emotional resilience.

Peter's saying also emphasises that God distributes his gifts *purposefully*; they are given "to serve others." They are not for self-indulgent pleasure but for altruistic ministry. We can always tell whether a so-called gift is from God by asking how much it benefits other people. If it parades or indulges ourselves, it is hardly a God-inspired gift.

The gifts of God are distributed *accountably*. They must be faithfully administered, Peter says. In other words, it is not simply a question of discerning and using the gift God has given, but of exercising it in a diligent, responsible and effective manner, recognising that we are stewards of his gifts and will one day have to give an account of how we have exercised our stewardship. It is tragic if a gifted person misuses the gift by exercising it lazily, boringly, arrogantly, selfishly or assertively.

Instead of doing the lowliest or highest things for the glory of Christ, they can be done with unworthy motives. Service can be spoiled by sin. The seventeenth-century Quaker, James Nayler, said, "The greatest and best gifts a man may receive from God are accompanied with the chiefest and worst temptations." That takes us to the next thing these great Christians are saying to us.

ACKNOWLEDGE OUR VULNERABILITY

Each of these spiritual classics emphasises what the Puritans used to call "the exceeding sinfulness of sin." In Augustine's experience we see that sin infects the mind, making us arrogant, independent, even rebellious towards God. Luther lingers with Paul's exposure in Romans 1:21 ("neither were thankful"), emphasising that sin expresses itself in human ingratitude and persistent idolatry, especially the idolisation of self. For Bunyan, sin clothes itself in persistent unbelief, humanity's stubborn resistance to what God has clearly said. For Wesley, there was no greater sin than lovelessness, the selfish refusal to devote our lives wholeheartedly to God and compassionately to others.

James Nayler knew the danger: "The soul is not safe while sin lives"; and we do well to heed the warning. None of our writers imagined that once they came to personal faith, sin could trouble them no more. They knew that the enemy continues his destructive work but often appears in a different guise. Augustine did not leave pride behind in that Milan garden, and Luther told his barber that the devil is always active. Wesley was ever alert to the enemy's changing strategy, but perhaps Bunyan described the devil's work with the greatest clarity. He was tempted not about sordid things, but about the best things in life, as during his daily communion with God and his fellowship with fellow Christians. The devil taunted him if he prayed, when he worshipped and as he preached.

There is no experience of the Christian life that removes from us the possibility of falling. All of us need to come to God afresh every day, seeking the power to live at our best for him. God promises the moral dynamic we need, Christ exemplifies it, and the Holy Spirit imparts it by his indwelling and empowering presence.

RENEW OUR DEPENDENCE

The central theme that comes through in each of these four books is that of the believer's total reliance on God. Spirituality is impossible without discipline, but discipline is not an exercise in self-effort. This divinely energised grace is the art of clinging closely to God every day. It grasps every opportunity to claim the promise of God's word, follow obediently in the steps of Christ and trust the illimitable resources of the Holy Spirit. God never demands the impossible, so the realisation of biblical ideals must be attainable, and our four writers offer some important clues as to how we may grow in spiritual maturity.

Augustine proclaims the sufficiency of God. His God has never failed to provide the resources for whatever he requires the believer to do; therefore, God can demand whatever he wishes: "Grant what you command, and command what you will." The strength is guaranteed. Inspired by the promise of Isaiah 46:4, Augustine adores the God who carries his people: " . . . you put us on your way, bringing comfort and saying: 'Run, I will carry you, and I will see you through to the end, and there I will carry you.'"[9]

Luther affirms the priority of prayer. He too maintains that Christians are "carried on the shoulders of Christ,"[10] but a truth like that must be appropriated in prayer. Our personal communion with God is the means whereby we express our need and the channel through which divine grace is mediated to us. To ignore this essential source of help is to revert to the idolatry of self; something or someone other than God has been given a preeminent place.

Bunyan asserts the omnipotence of grace. There is a comforting realism about these writers. They know that there are times when we all fail God and disappoint ourselves by being less than we genuinely want to be. However badly we fall, there is always a way back. The sensitive Bedford pastor knows that if we are genuinely penitent, sin will always be forgiven. Christ's "in no wise" means we will never be thrust away (Jn 6:37). Divine mercy covers the sin of any offender and defies the eloquence of every preacher: "God had a bigger mouth to speak with, than I had heart to conceive with."[11]

Bunyan rightly insists that there is an indestructible objectivity about the believer's relationship with God; our righteousness is in Christ, and it is not improved by our moral achievements nor damaged by our spiritual failures. It is "in heaven," secure in Christ, procured for us by his saving death upon the cross, and guaranteed as eternally effective by his unique resurrection.

Wesley declares the supremacy of love, and says two things about it. First, it is responsive love, loving God because he has first loved us. Only through that undeserved compassionate initiative can we be delivered from self-gratifying loving. Without a heart of love even religious ideals and service become painfully egocentric. Maldwyn Edwards said that before Aldersgate Street, Wesley "was continually asking what he could do; afterwards he only asked what God could do for him."[12]

It is also expulsive love, a love that displaces self-exaltation and challenges our allegiance to anything that deflects us from the highest and best. This was the love that roused Wesley in the early morning and thrust him out on his tireless journeys to proclaim its universality to others and to express its reality in persuasive words, practical deeds and courageous suffering. His greatest ambition was that he might "every sacred moment spend, in publishing the sinner's friend," living each day "as one who knows this life to be the seed-time of an eternal harvest."[13] Here is a love that adores God, serves others and is honoured to carry a cross. Those who so love give everything. On his thirty-eighth birthday Charles Wesley expressed that surrender in renewed commitment:

> *In a rapture of joy*
> *My life I employ,*
> *The God of my life to proclaim;*
> *'Tis worth living for this,*
> *To administer bliss*
> *And salvation in Jesus' name.*
>
> *My remnant of days*
> *I spend in his praise,*
> *Who died the whole world to redeem;*
> *Be they many or few,*
> *My days are his due,*
> *And they all are devoted to him.*

NOTES

INTRODUCTION

1. George Herbert, *A Priest to the Temple, or The Country Parson* (1675), chapter 4, p. 12.
2. Richard Baxter, *Dying Thoughts upon Phil 1:23,* 2nd ed. (1688), pp. 223-224.

AUGUSTINE

Unless otherwise stated, all references in this chapter are to *Saint Augustine: Confessions* (translated by Henry Chadwick), Oxford University Press, 1991. The numerals refer to books, chapters and paragraphs.

1. I i (1).
2. VIII viii (19); my italics.
3. I v (5) and (6).
4. I i (1); ii (2); iv (4); v (5).
5. III v (9).
6. VIII xii (29).
7. Letter 21 in *St. Augustine: Letters,* Vol. I (New York: Fathers of the Church, 1951), p. 48.
8. I vi (7).
9. VI v (8).
10. V i (1); ii (2) Augustine quotes from Psalm 19:6.
11. II vii (15); my italics.
12. II vii (15).
13. II i (1); ii (2).
14. VI v (8); vi (9).
15. X iii (3).
16. X iii (4).
17. I i (1).
18. X xliii (68) and (69).

19. X xxxvi (59).

20. IV xii (19).

21. VII xviii (24).

22. II iv (9)—ix (17).

23. Henry Chadwick, trans., *Saint Augustine: Confessions* (Oxford: Oxford University Press, 1991), p. 3.

24. I v (5).

25. I xviii (28).

26. II x (18).

27. III i (1).

28. IV xii (18).

29. III iv (7); my italics.

30. III vi (10) cf Isaiah 29:8.

31. XIII i (1).

32. Augustine, *Soliloquies*, Book I.24, ed. Gerard Watson (Warminster: Aris and Phillips, 1990), p. 59.

33. VII viii (12).

34. II v (10)—vi (13).

35. Augustine, *Expositions on the Book of Psalms*, Vol. 6 (Oxford: Library of the Fathers, 1857), p. 119.

36. Letter 24 in *St. Augustine: Letters*, Vol. 1 (New York: The Fathers of the Church, Vol. 12, 1951), p. 66; for Augustine's appreciation of friendship, see *Confessions*, IV viii (13)—ix (14).

37. I ix (14).

38. III iii (6).

39. VI viii (13).

40. IX viii (17) and (18).

41. IX viii (19).

42. III xi (19)—xii (21).

43. V viii (15).

44. IX x (23) and (24); xii (29) and (31).

45. IV iv (7)—ix (14).

46. V iii (3)—vii (13).

47. V viii (14) and (15).

48. V xiii (23); my italics.

49. V xiv (24) and (25).

50. VI xi (18).

51. VIII ii (4)—v (10).
52. VIII vi (13)—vii (16).

MARTIN LUTHER

The translation of Luther's *A Simple Way to Pray* used in this chapter is taken from *The Minister's Prayer Book*, edited by John W. Doberstein (London: Collins, 1964), pp. 437-60. It is also found in the American Edition of *Luther's Works*, Vol. 43 (Philadelphia: Fortress Press, 1968); an abbreviated version is in Theodore G. Tappert, *Luther: Letters of Spiritual Counsel*, Library of Christian Classics, Vol. 18 (London: SCM Press, 1955), pp. 124-30.

1. Luther, *Letters*, Vol. 1, American Edition of *Luther's Works*, Vol. 48 (Philadelphia: Fortress Press, 1963), p. 257. The letter is dated 13 July 1521.

2. *Martin Luther: Commentary on the Epistle to the Galatians*, revised translation by Philip S. Watson (Edinburgh: James Clarke, 1953), p. 333. (Galatians 3:23).

3. *Ibid.*, Preface, p. 16.

4. Luther, *Table Talk*. American Edition of *Luther's Works*, Vol. 54 (Philadelphia: Fortress Press, 1967), p. 155.

5. Luther, *A Letter of Consolation to All Who Suffer Persecution*. American Edition of *Luther's Works*, Vol. 43 (Philadelphia: Fortress Press, 1968), pp. 62-63.

6. Letter to Wenzeslaus Link, 10 July 1518. For this translation I am indebted to James Atkinson, *The Darkness of Faith: Daily Readings with Martin Luther* (London: Darton, Longman and Todd, 1987), p. 14.

7. Luther, *A Letter of Consolation*, p. 63.

8. Luther, *Lectures on Romans*, Library of Christian Classics, Vol. 15 (London: SCM Press, 1961), p. 91. (Romans 3:11).

9. Karl Holl, quoted by Gordon Rupp, *The Righteousness of God* (London: Hodder & Stoughton, 1953), p. 182.

10. Luther, *Lectures on Zechariah*. American Edition of *Luther's Works*, Vol. 20 (St Louis: Concordia, 1973), p. 80. (Zechariah 7:13).

11. Gordon Rupp, *The Righteousness of God*, p. 162; Luther, *Lectures on Romans*, pp. 25-26. (Romans 1:21-23).

12. Luther, *Lectures on Romans*, pp. 222, 225. (Romans 8:3).

13. Luther, *Commentary on Galatians*, pp. 179-80.

14. Joseph Lortz, *The Reformation in Germany*, English translation, Vol. 1 (London: Darton, Longman and Todd, 1968), p. 435.

15. Friedrich Heiler, *Prayer: A Study in the History and Psychology of Religion* (London: Oxford University Press, 1958), p. 119.

JOHN BUNYAN

Unless otherwise stated, all the references are to the numbered *paragraphs* in Bunyan's *Grace Abounding*. Throughout this chapter I have used a modern edition edited by W. R. Owens (Harmondsworth: Penguin Classics, 1987). Readers who would like to study the original text are referred to the Clarendon Press edition by Roger Sharrock (Oxford, 1962).

1. *Miscellaneous Works of John Bunyan*, Vol. 6, *The Poems*, ed. Graham Midgley (Oxford: Clarendon Press, 1980), vv. 4 and 5, p. 43.

2. 41.

3. 46.

4. R. S. Wallace, *Calvin's Doctrine of the Christian Life* (Edinburgh: Oliver and Boyd, 1959), pp. 87-93, 218-225.

5. Richard Sibbes, *Works of Richard Sibbes*, Vol. 4, ed. A. B. Grosart (London, 1862), pp. 213, 241.

6. Frances Ridley Havergal, *Memorials*, 2nd ed. (London, 1881), pp. 273-277.

7. *Confessions*, IV i (1).

8. Preface to *Grace Abounding*.

9. *Reliquiae Baxterianae* (The Autobiography of Richard Baxter), I, 1, Everyman Edition (London, 1931), p. 11.

10. 12.

11. 58-60.

12. 66.

13. 96.

14. 97.

15. 98.

16. 102-104.

17. 131-141.

18. W. E. Sangster, *A Spiritual Check-up* (London: Epworth Press, 1952); see also the same author's *The Secret of Radiant Life* (London: Hodder and Stoughton, 1957), especially Part II, "The Person I Am."

19. 26-27.

20. 37.

21. 32.

22. 238-243.

23. 105.

24. J. Horsfall Turner, ed., *Rev. Oliver Heywood Autobiography*, Vol. 1 (Brighouse, 1882-5), p. 58; Oliver Sansom, *A Short Account of Many Remarkable Passages in the Life of Oliver Sansom* (London, 1710), p. 2.

25. 29.

26. 46.

27. 22, 204, 260.

28. 49, 153, 270.

29. 93-94.

30. 173.

31. 208.

32. 204-205.

33. 206-214.

34. 215-216.

35. 37-38.

36. 74, 53-55.

37. 46.

38. 77.

39. 79.

40. 184.

41. 164.

42. 180.

43. 117.

44. 179.

45. Arthur Dent, *The Plain Man's Pathway to Heaven* (London, 1601), pp. 15-16.

46. Lewis Bayly, *The Practice of Piety* (London, 1632), pp. 238-244. This practice of "occasional meditation" is also developed in Thomas Gouge, *The Young Man's Guide*; William Spurstow, *The Spiritual Chymist*; and Richard Baxter, *The Saint's Everlasting Rest*.

47. 142-144.

48. 129-130.

49. Richard J. Foster and James Bryan Smith, eds., *Devotional Classics: Selected Readings for Individuals and Groups*, revised ed. (London: Hodder and Stoughton, 1993).

50. 84-92.

51. Preface.

52. 339.

53. 244, cf. 16-19, 30-32.

54. 321.

55. Conclusion, 5.

56. 235, 245, 321, 323.

57. 255-260.

58. 333-337.

59. 322.

JOHN WESLEY

Unless otherwise stated, all the references are to the dates in Wesley's *Journal*, Standard Edition, N. Curnock, ed. (London: Epworth, 1938), 8 vols.

1. Adam Clarke, *Memoirs of the Wesley Family* (London, 1823), p. 94.

2. 28 June 1770.

3. 24 May 1738.

4. Augustine Birrell, *Collected Essays and Addresses*, Vol. 1 (London, 1922), pp. 308-309.

5. For an account of the satiric reaction to eighteenth-century Methodism, with chapters on Wesley, Whitefield and their colleagues in the societies, see Albert M. Lyles, *Methodism Mocked* (London: Epworth, 1960).

6. 19 July 1749.

7. J. Telford, ed., *Letters of John Wesley* (London: Epworth, 1932) Vols. 3: 212; 5: 315, 333; 6:116 (hereafter *Letters*).

8. Ibid., 7: 90.

9. Ibid., 3:137, 213; 7:102.

10. Ibid., 3:221; 4:10.

11. 27 August 1768.

12. *Letters*, 4:297-300.

13. Ibid., 6:42.

14. Wesley, Sermon CVI, On Faith in *Works*, ed. T. Jackson, Vol. 7 (London, 1872; reprinted Grand Rapids: Zondervan), p. 202.

15. 17-18 February 1751.

16. 31 July 1753.

17. 20-22 October 1753.

18. 15-16 February 1747.

19. 19 May 1753.

20. 25 June 1749; see also 20 May 1752, 9 October 1755.

21. 22 March 1752.

22. 11 October 1752.

23. 16 December 1755.

24. 4 January 1754.

25. 21 March 1756.

26. 16 September 1739.

27. Quoted in D. Dunn Wilson, *Many Waters Cannot Quench* (London: Epworth, 1969), p. 29. Dr. Dunn Wilson's book is a sensitive exposition of the nature, range and theology of Methodist suffering in this period.

28. Thomas Jackson, ed., *The Journal of the Rev. Charles Wesley* (London, 1849), 5 February 1747.

29. 18 February 1744.

30. 18-22 June 1743.

31. 20 October 1743.

32. John Wesley, "A Short History of the People called Methodists" in *Works*, Vol. 13 (London, 1872), pp. 307-308.

33. 31 March—2 April 1739.

34. 11 June 1739.

35. 1 April 1739.

36. 27 April 1761.

37. 20 May 1759.

38. 6 September 1772.

39. *Boswell's Life of Johnson*, Vol. 3 (Oxford: Clarendon, 1934), 230 (31 March 1778).

40. *Letters*, 5: 344.

41. 1 August 1742.

42. *Letters*, 8: 211.

43. 29-30 August, 2 September 1759.

44. 9 September 1759.

45. 13 June 1739; see also 21 December 1751.

46. 16 January 1760.

47. 25 July 1753.

48. 23 June 1759.

49. 21 September 1762.

50. 25 November 1740.

51. 15 October 1759.

52. *Letters*, 8:265.

53. 3 November 1740.

54. 8 February 1753.

55. 7 May 1741.

CONCLUSION

1. *Grace Abounding*, Preface.

2. *Confessions*, I xx (31); II vii (15); III xi (19); VI xvi (26).

3. William Haller, *The Rise of Puritanism* (New York: Harper, 1957), pp. 96-97.

4. For the spiritual impact of this neglected literature, see Leslie F. Church, *The Early Methodist People* (London: Epworth, 1948), and *More About the Early Methodist People* (London: Epworth, 1949).

5. Edward England, ed., *Keeping a Spiritual Journal* (Crowborough: Highland Books, 1988).

6. For these collections of prayers see F. C. Gill, *John Wesley's Prayers* (London: Epworth, 1951).

7. *Spiritual Letters of Archbishop Fenelon: Letters to Women*, trans. H. L. Lear (London, 1877), pp. 21-22.

8. *Grace Abounding*, paragraphs 107, 110.

9. *Confessions*, X xxix (40); VI xvi (26).

10. *Luther's Works: Lectures on Philemon, Titus and Hebrews*, American Edition, Vol. 29 (St Louis, Missouri: Concordia, 1968), p. 226.

11. *Grace Abounding*, paragraph 249.

12. Maldwyn Edwards, *The Astonishing Youth: A Study of John Wesley as Men Saw Him* (London: Epworth, 1959), p. 80.

13. F. C. Gill, *John Wesley's Prayers*, p. 45.